Pra
The Box

"In a world that still stigmatizes mental illness, it's beyond refreshing to see someone share their journey through decades of anxiety with such openness and honesty. And that's exactly what Wendy Tamis Robbins does in *The Box*. She bears it all, from her generalized and social anxiety and phobias to her eating disorder and suicidal thoughts and proves that regaining control of your life IS possible. And that's such an impactful and necessary message in today's world because too many people are living as prisoners of their anxiety. Her powerful and relatable memoir is proof to anyone suffering with debilitating anxiety that there is life beyond their mental illness. Robbins is so real about how her refusal to keep her anxieties hidden ultimately changed her life. And that makes *The Box* a must-read for anyone who's been silently struggling with mental illness out of fear that there's no hope for change. Because Wendy proves that change IS possible when you choose to take control of your disorder and live your life with resilience."

—Lisa Sugarman,
nationally syndicated columnist, radio show host, and author of
How To Raise Perfectly Imperfect Kids And Be Ok With It,
Untying Parent Anxiety, and *LIFE: It Is What It Is*

"This book is a love letter to anyone who's ever struggled to understand—and find hope—while dealing with the loneliness and frustration of anxiety."

—Brenda Ockun,
StepMom Magazine, Founder/Publisher

THE BOX

An Invitation to
Freedom From
Anxiety

Wendy Tamis Robbins

MADE FOR
SUCCESS

Made for Success Publishing
P.O. Box 1775 Issaquah, WA 98027
www.MadeForSuccessPublishing.com

Distributed by Made for Success Publishing

First Printing

Library of Congress Cataloging-in-Publication data
Tamis Robbins, Wendy
    THE BOX: An Invitation to Freedom from Anxiety
        p. cm.

LCCN: 2021934739

ISBN: 978-1-64146-622-6 (*Paperback*)
ISBN: 978-1-64146-634-9 (*Audiobook*)
ISBN: 978-1-64146-633-2 (*eBook*)

Printed in the United States of America

For further information contact Made for Success Publishing
+14255266480 or email service@madeforsuccess.net

Contents

Note from the Author

I am no longer the 6-year-old hiding in a cardboard box, or the 30-year-old paralyzed with anxiety, or the 35-year-old asking for a divorce. They are important parts of my journey but belong in the past. I am now the observer and the witness giving them a voice.

This book is quasi-autobiographical. The stories I tell are what I believe happened at some point in my life to some version of my former self. However, those who experienced these events alongside me, as protagonists, friends, saviors, or mere witnesses, likely have different versions of how these events played out because they experienced and internalized them in their own unique way. What I saw, heard, and felt is what I witnessed and my truth. Parts of my story may have only existed in my mind, while other parts may be what I want to believe or wish had happened. These chapters do not attempt to paint an accurate depiction of historical events, but rather to reflect what I have carried with me and been defined by until now.

Preface

My ANXIETY STARTED as a young child and ebbed and flowed for over 40 years. What I didn't know then was that anxiety disorders affect 25 percent of children between the ages of 13 and 18 years old. They also often co-occur with other disorders such as depression, obsessive-compulsive disorder (OCD), and eating disorders.[1]

Collecting more disorders as my anxiety progressed was certainly my experience. I had a little bit of everything, and, at times, a lot of one thing or another. I had social anxiety, generalized anxiety, health anxiety, panic disorder, intrusive thoughts, harm OCD, depression caused by chronic anxiety, depersonalization and derealization disorder, and eating disorders woven throughout. I went untreated until adulthood, and even then, I was under-diagnosed, and treatment was not very effective.

All of these mental health issues created a desperate sense of isolation. I wish I had known then what I know for sure now: I am not alone. According to the Anxiety and Depression Association of America (ADAA), anxiety-related disorders are the most common mental illness in the United States, affecting more than 40 million adults age 18 and older every year. That is over 18 percent of the population. These disorders develop from a complex set of risk factors, including genetics, brain chemistry, personality, and life events.

Nearly one-half of those diagnosed with depression are also diagnosed with an anxiety disorder.[2]

Even those who don't suffer from a disorder have experienced anxiety in one form or another. It is a normal human reaction to a stressful situation. Actually, it is considered a beneficial response in certain dangerous situations that trigger our fight-or-flight response, and the physical symptoms are coming from our autonomic nervous system.[3] Our lives provide countless opportunities to experience normal anxiety: exams, relationships, illness, jobs, pandemics, elections, and civil unrest are just the tip of the iceberg. This "normal" anxiety is generally fleeting.

When anxiety becomes more constant and intense, it becomes a problem. The definition of generalized anxiety disorder is: "The presence of excessive anxiety and worry about a variety of topics, events, or activities. Worry occurs more often than not for at least six months and is clearly excessive," according to the Diagnostic and Statistical Manual of Mental Disorders, Fifth Edition published by the American Psychiatric Association. Generalized anxiety disorder, or GAD, affects 6.8 million adults, or 3.1 percent of the U.S. population. Women are twice as likely to be affected as men.[4]

Panic disorder affects 6 million adults, or 2.7 percent of the U.S. population. Again, women are twice as likely to be affected as men.[5]

Social anxiety disorder, or SAD, affects 15 million adults, or 6.8 percent of the U.S. population. SAD is equally common among men and women and typically begins around age 13.[6]

OCD affects 2.2 million adults, or 1 percent of the U.S. population. OCD is equally common among men and women. The average age of onset is 19, with 25 percent of cases occurring by age 14. One-third of affected adults first experienced symptoms in childhood.[7]

A group that is particularly at risk is college students. Unfortunately, no one prepared me, mentally or emotionally, for the transition from the complete familiarity and comfort of my hometown, my family and friends, known expectations and dangers, to a completely foreign environment, full of strangers, unrealistic expectations, and unknown threats. This was in large part because neither my parents nor my teachers or advisors knew about these statistics or were aware of my underlying disorder. Nor were there adequate services at the time to diagnose and deal with such issues. Since that time, I have seen countless college students battle new and/or exacerbated mental health issues and struggle to get the help they need. Some experience them for the first time and don't know how to handle them. Others find that certain thoughts and feelings that were just surfacing in high school take hold and gain momentum. Meanwhile, others hear an old, familiar voice and feel a sense of dread that casts an unwelcome shadow over what should be an exciting new adventure.

In an article published on March 19, 2018, *Time Magazine* reported on the record number of college students who are seeking treatment for depression and anxiety. The Center for Collegiate Mental Health found in a 2015 report that between 2009 and 2015, the number of students visiting counseling centers increased by about 30 percent on average, while enrollment grew by less than 6 percent. Students seeking help are increasingly likely to have attempted suicide or engaged in self-harm, the center found. The director of Boston University's Center for Anxiety & Related Disorders and a College of Arts & Sciences clinical associate professor of psychological and brain sciences, Lisa Smith, said, "We know that stress can be a trigger of psychological conditions, especially in the context of unpredictability and uncontrollability. This seems to be inherent in the transition to college."

Which leads me to the most frightening statistic—suicide is the second-leading cause of death for people ages 10–34 (the 10th leading cause of death in the U.S. overall).[8] And, more than 90 percent of people who die by suicide show symptoms of a mental health condition.[9]

Finally, both depersonalization and derealization disorder (DP and DR, respectively) are lesser-known conditions that I didn't even know existed when I was experiencing them. They are categorized by the National Alliance on Mental Illness as dissociative disorders, which are characterized by an involuntary escape from reality caused by a disconnection between one's thoughts, identity, consciousness, and memory. It's estimated that "up to 75% of people experience at least one depersonalization/derealization episode in their lives, with only 2% meeting the full criteria for chronic episodes" according to the National Alliance on Mental Illness, including all age groups and racial, ethnic, and socioeconomic backgrounds. Again, women are more likely than men to be diagnosed.[10]

The symptoms of a dissociative disorder usually first develop as a response to a traumatic event, such as abuse or military combat, to keep those memories under control. However, DP and DR can also occur as a symptom of chronic or severe anxiety, and experts agree that it is not dangerous and is likely to be a coping mechanism for the brain.[11] Many people in this state of anxiety already fear they are going crazy and losing touch with reality, so this state of mind can exacerbate that fear, causing even more anxiety, depression, and thoughts of suicide. While the quickest way back to reality is to de-escalate the anxiety and panic, which means meeting the dissociative feelings with calm and acceptance, this can be extremely challenging for someone struggling with it.[12]

DP involves ongoing feelings of detachment from your actions, feelings, thoughts, and sensations as if you are watching a movie as an outside observer of those thoughts and feelings, and even your body. People can feel like a robot, not in control of their speech or movements. They can experience emotional or physical numbness of their senses or responses to the world around them.[13]

While DR is similar in ways, it is less about the person's own body and mind and more about their surroundings. For example, it may seem like other people and things in the world around them are unreal. They can feel alienated from or unfamiliar with their environment—again, like they are living in a movie or a dream. They can feel emotionally disconnected from people they care about, as if they were separated by a glass wall. Surroundings can appear distorted, blurry, colorless, two-dimensional or artificial, and time can be distorted, such as recent events feeling like the distant past.[14]

I experienced both at the same time to varying degrees, and while some may suffer symptoms for just a matter of moments, mine swallowed months of my life at times. The average onset age is 16, although DP episodes can start anywhere from early- to mid-childhood.[15]

As I try to pinpoint where my anxiety originated, I see genetic and environmental factors. I also see a collection of auto-immune disorders. First, I was diagnosed with Hashimoto's disease (thyroid), then psoriasis—with intense flare-ups during particularly stressful periods. Then I experienced early-onset hearing loss with resulting and constant tinnitus. These conditions also suggest a higher proclivity for anxiety. So, whether it was caused by genes, environment, trauma, body chemistry, high intelligence, or most likely a little bit of each, I've also had to treat them with a little bit of everything.

All of this knowledge has come to me after many decades of living with these disorders. While you are in the fire, it is very difficult to internalize statistics or descriptions. Awareness and separation are required in order to view it in an intellectual rather than emotional way. But when you can do that, it can be transformational. When you finally understand the chemistry, the external factors, and the commonality, you are relieved of the burden that you are at fault and broken beyond repair.

Purpose

"She must find a boat and sail in it.
No guarantee of shore.
Only a conviction that what she wanted could exist,
if she dared to find it."
—Jeanette Winterson

I BELIEVE THE HIGHEST purpose for each of us is to realize our fullest potential by living our most authentic life—unapologetically, in color, and out loud. But we all face barriers between imagining what that life looks like and then actually living it. Those barriers come in all shapes and sizes. Some are mere hurdles, while others are brick walls. *These* are the boxes we find ourselves in.

We started building them at different times and for different reasons. We had different tools at our disposal. The world can be an overwhelming and unpredictable place, and we use these coping mechanisms and mental constructs to deal with and make sense of it all. Some are healthy, and some are destructive. Just as each person's journey is unique, so are the boxes we live in.

As a child, I was overwhelmed by my fears and began building walls to protect myself from what caused them. As I grew, my fears grew irrational and all-consuming, manifesting into an anxiety and panic disorder with isolated bouts of depression. As the anxiety escalated, my walls grew taller and thicker. I watched my world shrinking around me. What was once my safe place had become my prison. The limitations I had placed on my life, both physically and mentally, were literally suffocating me.

My journey out of my box wasn't a place I could pin on a map and sail to. My journey was within. In order to heal and grow, I had to revisit open wounds and process my pain. In order to climb up those walls and out of that box, I first had to go down and back. Deep down and *way* back.

I set out to find the source of my anxiety in order to understand and find the strength to overcome it. In revisiting my past experiences and traumas with more awareness, I could see them more clearly and understand how they affected me on a deeper level. I needed to see them through the eyes of a terrified little girl hiding in a cardboard box. I had to feel her hyperventilating and grasping onto life so painfully tight that it was slipping through her fingers—and I had to give her the comfort she desperately needed. I needed to be her safety, her lifeline. And I needed to show her that it can be different. Because ultimately, it *is* different. By going back to save her, I saved myself.

This is how I overcame the debilitating anxiety that kept me from realizing my fullest potential and living my most authentic life. This is my hero's journey.

Even after so much work has been done, there are still dragons to slay and treasures to find. Every day, I challenge myself not only to rewrite the end of my story, but to reframe my past, not as a life of limitations, missed opportunities, and failures, but rather as a life of courage and triumph, reconciliation, and redemption.

Once I finally decided to change my life, it wasn't as easy as opening my eyes to the box I was living in, finding the door, and walking out into the life I'd always dreamed of. The journey has been the most challenging and transformative of my life. But I found my way out, and so can you.

What is this book about?

I am not a psychiatrist, and this is not a self-help book. I am a lawyer, and this is a memoir. I've suffered with an anxiety disorder since I was 7 years old, and while I benefited from psychiatrists and self-help books along the way, they always fell short for me.

My psychiatrists had degrees and prescription pads but lacked personal experience. They were always on the outside looking in. Self-help books offered recipes for success in seven simple steps but lacked a personal connection. I found it nearly impossible to internalize their advice and implement their techniques while in the cauldron of panic and pain. And even when I had the clarity to do so, they focused on managing my symptoms, not overcoming my disorder, which, to me, meant forever limiting my life to accommodate it. I was left feeling helpless and hopeless.

While my anxiety and bouts with depression looked and felt different at various times in my life, I needed to hear the stories on these pages at every point on my path. I needed to know I wasn't alone. I needed to be reminded of who I was and what I was capable of. I needed to hear that there was hope—hope that I could find my way out and reclaim my life.

This book chronicles my journey to overcome the debilitating anxiety that kept me from realizing my full potential and living my most authentic life—a life with deep, emotional connections, a life of adventure and risk-taking, a life full of wonder and curiosity and saying "yes," a life lived on my own terms, based on my own dreams and desires, not based on my diagnosis.

Is this book for you?

If you saw the word "anxiety" on the book jacket and picked it up, then this book is for you. I wrote it with you in mind. Maybe you suffer in the shadows, clenching a pill in one hand and a coffee in the other, desperately trying to look happy and in control, but unraveling inside. Whether you've just recently been introduced to the crippling effects of anxiety or you can hardly remember life before anxiety, these stories will resonate. They shine a light in those dark spaces and show you that this very struggle can be your greatest source of strength.

Maybe it's not anxiety but something else that has kept you from living your best life. I wrote this book for you, too. If you used to call yourself a dreamer and now your dreams follow you around in fragments on the floor, rattling like cans hanging off a bumper, reminding you of empty promises you made to yourself and never kept, then this book is for you.

Or maybe it's not you who is suffering. Maybe you've never felt anything but normal twinges of anxiety and moved on unaffected. But now, you find yourself completely helpless as you watch your son or daughter or loved one struggle with mental illness. I wrote this book to pull you into their world and show you a glimpse of their suffering so you can start the conversation, ask the questions you've been avoiding, and maybe even save a life.

This book is a raw and honest depiction of what life looks and feels like under the cloak of constant anxiety and the fear of reoccurring bouts of depression. The chapters stand on their own as a story or lesson, each building on the last as the path is revealed. Coupled with inspirational quotes, sobering statistics, poems that were written in the trenches, and surreal narratives written in prose that will take the reader on a journey of empowerment, reconciliation, emotional transformation, spiritual redemption, and self-love.

Part One begins in the environment that triggered my first anxious thoughts and my need to control every situation and outcome—and laid the foundation for the walls to come. Part Two continues through years of living in the box with all of its limitations and restrictions, missed opportunities and struggles, until I realize that I created my own prison. These walls were not providing protection, only pain. I was no longer in control of my life. Anxiety controlled everything.

Part Three reveals how and why I made the decision to find my way out, even without an obvious path or guaranteed outcome. The stories in these chapters illustrate how I navigated that transformative process through deepened self-awareness and expanded consciousness. Part Four culminates in revealing the life I have manifested on the outside of my box.

Why should you take this journey with me?

I had my first panic attack when I was just 7 years old. I have experienced anxiety first-hand from the time I can remember having any thoughts. I have hit rock bottom and found my way back out to a life I never thought possible. I understand the perspective from both places now. I know what it feels like to be one step away from being swallowed by the darkness and the strength needed to take one more step toward the light. I challenged the conventions that told me I had to manage my symptoms, as it was not possible to leave them behind.

I discovered that after trying it all—various therapies, prescription drugs, alcohol, self-help books, meditation, yoga, prayer, diet, and even a loving partner—it is possible. But not just with any one of them. I needed all of them and much more. I took one small step at a time and watched as the path revealed itself to me along the way. This path led me to the treasure that had been buried deep inside of me all along. And I can honestly say that I am the strongest I've ever been. I can honestly say that I love myself, every part—even the crazy thoughts—because now I know where they came from.

While writing this book, I tapped into my over 20 years of experience as an attorney, processing complex ideas, to navigate these similarly complex mental and emotional constructs. I then added proper context and vivid imagery to communicate them intimately and effectively. It may be difficult to walk this path with me at times, but I would encourage you, in those moments, to take a step back and view my story through your own lens. I hope it will help you reach a deeper understanding of the labor of your journey.

Why did I write this book?

For me, hearing personal stories was integral to finding initial relief from the isolation anxiety created and the fear that I was losing my mind. I promise that as you take this journey with me, you won't feel alone. My stories will draw you into spaces you may have never shared or revealed to anyone.

When you see and feel me go through these very personal experiences, you will see and feel yourself or your loved one go through them as well. These stories offer hope that you can heal, that you can find the strength to overcome your obstacles, and ultimately, that you will be empowered to rewrite the ending of your own story.

After having struggled with anxiety for almost 40 years, I felt like I was carrying two bags—one full of fear and panic and another full of the tools I'd collected to manage them. They weighed me down and held me back from fully embracing and living my life.

I was tired of making concessions and excuses. I could feel myself fading into the background of my own world. I was losing myself. I needed to know if I could ever drop the bags, unclench my hands, and spread my arms wide to take flight again.

I know now that if you do the inner work, the anxious mind can be quieted and redirected to guide you to your sacred path that leads you back home to a place of pure, inner peace and self-love. I can tell you with confidence that it is possible to see yourself, describe yourself, and even define yourself as a person who no longer suffers from an anxiety disorder.

I wrote this book as a way to make sense of my pain and give it purpose. That purpose is to help you find your own way out. Other than a few family members and friends, all of whom I could count on one hand, no one knows that I suffered from anxiety or had bouts of depression. So, to expose it in such a public way is in service to you, the reader, the version of me that was searching for answers and hope that things could be different.

I hope you see my tears on these pages as your eyes well up and you find a path to heal and reclaim your life. And when you see that I have traded constant fear and dread for courage and resilience, that I am now living an empowered life without limits, that I am free to follow my sacred path to peace, happiness, and true connection, you will see that all of that can be true for you, too.

Introduction

*"No one can construct for you the bridge upon which
precisely you must cross the stream of life,
no one but you yourself alone."*
—Friedrich Nietzsche

YEARS AGO, a friend told me that if I look up at the stars long enough, they will begin to take shape, and in them, I'd find beautiful constellations. What once seemed like chaos suddenly makes perfect sense.

That night, I looked up at the sky and saw my anxious state reflected in the darkness—my mind shattered into a million pieces and scattered across the sky. The stars represented my thoughts, beliefs, dreams, fears, and memories. Looking at them all at once overwhelmed me. I saw only chaos, not order. They didn't make sense to me because *I* didn't make sense to me. All I knew was that they were all a part of me and had settled into my bones.

At the beginning of my journey, I didn't know how they were all related or connected. I was still just a passive observer, seeing only stars with no meaning and offering no direction. But what if I did the work to find the constellations? What if I sat with them long enough for the magic to happen? The magic when one star connects to another and another, and they begin to take form. What if I allowed the pieces of my puzzle to shift around inside of me as I sifted through the painful places, giving my fears a face and my shame a name? What if, over time, this opened my heart enough so the constellations became clear and the pieces of the puzzle fit together to reveal the picture I was always meant to see?

When I was first searching for a way to finally overcome my anxiety, I was talking with this friend about fear and my saboteurs. I described my loudest saboteur as a familiar voice that had been with me for many years. When that voice was loud and stern, telling me I was unsafe or unworthy, I was comfortable fighting back—at times. I would get bigger and louder and force it into the shadows where it became a mere whisper … until it inevitably resurfaced. But sometimes, the voice had a well-reasoned argument and brought me into the shadows with it. Either way, it was omnipresent.

Where was this voice coming from? Why couldn't I do things that others did with ease, things that excited and inspired me, that my spirit and soul longed for? The voice of my saboteur felt relentless and cunning, finding ways to hold me back and silence my authentic voice until I grew too tired to fight anymore.

I knew this voice was my fear talking, and I was choosing to let it take over my life and sit in the driver's seat. But it never felt like a choice. I was conscious it was happening, but it felt very much like it was happening *to* me and was completely out of my control. I couldn't remember handing over the keys because I didn't remember ever having them in the first place.

Over time, as I became better at recognizing and banishing the loud voice, the stronger the more imperceptible voice became. Like water finding its way through the tiniest cracks, it morphed to find another way in. That softer, quieter voice became my more challenging struggle. Just when I thought I was free and in control, this other voice crept under my skin without permission and seeped into my bones without me realizing it. It changed my thoughts, and I was unaware of the subtle shift. In the moment, I believed it was my own voice. It was a whisper on the wind during a beautiful walk in the woods telling me I'd gone too far and was dangerously lost. It was a convenient excuse to avoid going out in public because of a slight change in schedules or weather.

The loud saboteur demanded a sharp turn off my path. Sometimes I could clearly see what was happening in the moment and wept as I felt fear turning the wheel. A deep sense of disconnection from my true self grew inside me, but I could not control the anxiety, so I let it happen. But the softer, more subversive suggestions put into motion small shifts that over time led me down a path that I never consciously chose. The subtle nudging along the way was less perceivable but not any less painful when I looked up and wondered, "How did I get here?"

I needed to find the source of the fear, the dread, the panic, and the anxiety that was writing my story. And that meant I needed to identify my saboteur and understand its motivation.

That's when I saw the first line connect one star to another and had an overwhelming feeling that this was the first step on my journey—my journey out of the shadows and into the light, where I could find my truth and reclaim my life.

A few days after that discussion, I meditated on the voice of my saboteur. I described it to myself as strong, argumentative, persuasive, manipulative, and opportunistic. I remembered hearing it on beautiful warm days when it slithered through quiet, sacred spaces like a snake in the grass, reminding me that the calm I felt was fleeting and my momentary peace was undeserved. Or when I'd roll down the window of my car on that first spring day, and the moment I felt pure joy the voice reminded me of how easily I could die in a car accident. Or when I finally felt loved, and it convinced me that once my broken pieces were exposed, I would be shamed and abandoned.

Still meditating, a striking and unexpected image appeared to me. It was the Wizard of Oz. It was the actual large green head with fire blazing on either side of it. *What the hell is the Wizard of Oz doing in my meditation?* I thought. I remembered the lies it told and felt the rage it radiated. Then I remembered the rumors that surrounded the legend of the Wizard. That it could give you whatever you needed or were missing—a heart, a brain, some courage.

What was I missing? What did this mean? As the image and voices swirled through my head, I felt like I was getting nowhere. Then, suddenly, they found their way to my heart and moved me to pull back the curtain next to the Wizard. Standing there with her hands on the controls was a little girl shaking in fear. It was me. I knew in that moment the voice I'd been hearing since I was a child was hers.

Behind that big, bold voice was the fear of a little girl who had grown bigger in a world that was scarier than she could manage. I felt deep in my heart she was only acting out of fear, and her sole mission was to save me.

"What are you *doing?*" I asked.

"No questions. *I'm* in control here," she replied, still looking forward.

"Why do you need to be in control?"

"Because I'm ..." she paused. "I'm *terrified*," she said, turning toward me with tears streaming down her face. In that moment, I felt her fear rise to the surface and into every corner of my body. I understood in an instant why she needed to do everything in her power to control me for all of these years. She was terrified of being alone, abandoned, unloved, and unsafe, terrified of never being enough, never being accepted, never being able to save the people she loved, never feeling calm or at peace.

Then she looked at me and said, "I am terrified of leaving the box."

What box? I thought. *Where is this going?*

I took a deep breath in and suddenly remembered it—the box.

When I was growing up, my home life was chaotic and volatile at times. One of my favorite places to play and hide was a big cardboard box we got when my parents bought a new refrigerator. I loved spending time in that box because I knew only God and me could fit. But playing became hiding when I heard the muffled sounds of people yelling and dishes breaking outside those cardboard walls.

Since the moment she left that box, this little girl had become a master at trying to protect me from an unsafe world full of rage, tears, violence, and loneliness. So, she created a new, slightly bigger box for me and, over time, fortified those flimsy cardboard walls with materials meant to be pain-proof. And I sat by and watched as she extinguished my light and drowned me in a sea of anxiety.

Remembering all this, I realized that little girl had built these walls to protect her from failure, pain, rejection, abandonment, chaos, even death, and in doing so, had ignited and perpetuated this disorder. But if she held the key that kept me locked in, did she also hold the key to my escape?

I knew then that rejecting her was not the answer. I realized that the only way to get where I wanted to be was to embrace her. To show her the love and comfort she had been longing for since I was her age.

I had to go back into that box with compassion and make her trust me enough to leave with me. I took her hands off the controls and held them in mine, and together, we set out on our journey.

We would have to walk through those years together so that I could understand what she was trying to do for me and experience them all over again while loving and protecting her. In saving her in those moments, I would save myself. This was my path to reconciliation and my road to redemption. It was not a road I would follow on a map, but one I would feel in my heart.

In that moment, I was reminded of the chaotic sky and realized another line was drawn, from one star to another, revealing a little bit more of the picture and illuminating the next steps on my path.

Part 1

BUILDING THE BOX

Chapter 1

Hands to Heaven

"It is a happy talent to know how to play."
—Ralph Waldo Emerson

As A CHILD, I didn't so much play as I escaped. I hid myself away, collecting companions like dolls and acorns, all so willing to stay. I told them elaborate stories to distract myself until it was time again to go back. Back to the not knowing, but knowing too much to play.

You fall into play with a light heart; you escape with a heavy one. Play is open and endless, full of laughter and running with arms stretched wide open to capture the wind and the sun and pull them close until you are one. Escape is stolen moments, promises made to be broken, sitting with crossed arms and legs in the corners of closets and attics dreaming until the silence grows so loud it steals the next moment, and again, you go back because you have to. Because you know—too much, and too little.

I didn't play. I escaped. There is a difference.

Like most weekdays around that time, I was coloring at the kitchen table while my mom was cooking supper. I didn't know how to tell time yet, but I knew that when both arms were on the 5, it was time for my dad to be home. When the short arm was on the 5 and the long arm pointed straight to heaven, I moved to the kitchen to watch the back door. That's the door my dad came in. I looked at the door, then my coloring book, then my mom's face, and back around again. My mom did the same. She looked at food, then the door, then at me, and back around again.

When the long arm reached the 6, I stopped coloring. Bad butterflies started flying around in my stomach. I wanted to go to my room and hide, but I stayed to watch my mom and see if she started looking mad like the other times. If that happened, I would have to try to calm her down before bad things happened.

"Where is your father?" she asked me. She said it like she wasn't mad, but I could feel my muscles get tight, so I knew it was starting.

"He'll be home soon," I said. I prayed he was in traffic or had something left to do at work. She stared at the clock when the long arm reached the 7 and asked me again, only louder this time.

"He'll be home soon. He doesn't mean it," I said, breathing really fast as I watched the long arm move past the 7 and toward the 8. My mom walked around faster and faster and banged things louder and louder.

The long arm moved up the side of the clock painfully slow, like when I tried to walk up the sledding hill in my snowsuit and boots.

I think I even saw it rest on the 9 like I always did halfway up the hill. It was like God was giving my dad extra time. I started praying, "*God, please let him come home, please let him come home, please let him come home.*"

When the long arm finally pointed up to heaven again, my mom called my big sister to the kitchen table to eat dinner and put my little brother in his highchair. I watched my sister sit down and knew she didn't know what was happening. I couldn't eat. I held my breath, waiting for her to ask where Dad was. It was like waiting for a bomb to explode. I started thinking my dad was hurt because I knew he wouldn't come home late unless something terrible happened. He knew what happened when he was late, and he would never do that to me on purpose. I started watching the phone, waiting for it to ring and say Dad had been in a car accident and we needed to go see him in the hospital. Then I looked back at the door, scared of what would happen if he walked through it.

My eyes moved from the clock to the door to the phone then around again, never looking at my food. "Eat your dinner!" she yelled. My back got straight, and I grabbed my fork. "I didn't cook for an hour so I could throw it away!" she yelled again. I felt her getting increasingly angry and knew it was only going to get worse as that long arm fell back down to the 5. That would mean it went around the clock one whole time, and that would be *really* bad.

I moved the food around my plate as my muscles tightened and my stomach cramped. I wanted to cry, but I just kept my face still so my mom couldn't tell that I knew something was wrong. If I pretended like I didn't know, maybe she would forget. If I started to get upset, it might remind her to look at the clock again, and I couldn't do that to my dad.

I made it through about half of my pork chop when the long hand was on the 4 and I saw Dad walking toward the back door. I felt like I might throw up right there on the table. I dropped my fork and grabbed either side of my chair seat with both hands as hard as I could. When he reached for the doorknob, I took a deep breath and held it in. He had a big smile on his face like he missed me, but his eyes looked tired. I yelled, "Dad!" and before I let go of my chair, my mom was on him.

She yelled questions really close to his face. I saw water spraying off her and couldn't tell if it was spit or tears. He answered her questions and seemed confused when she got even madder. I knew something was different about him, but I didn't know what, and that made me more scared.

When the screaming got louder, I knew my pork chop wasn't going to matter anymore, so I ran. On my way up the stairs, I heard something smash on the floor, so I snuck back down and peeked around the corner. When the screaming started again, I ran back up to my room. My sister was already there. I was always the last to stay and watch them fight just in case one of them needed my help—like I could somehow make it better.

I sat on my bed crying, holding my head in my hands. My sister laid on her bed reading until we were both jolted by a hard knock on the door. I felt relieved that it might be Dad apologizing for not hugging me when he got home and, at the same time, terrified it might be her.

As I put my hand on the knob, the door flew open and smashed into the wall so hard the doorknob punched a hole in it. She was standing there, almost unrecognizable, her face red and swollen, crying in a way I'd only seen in babies. It was as if she had turned into a different person. She grabbed my shirt and dragged me into the bathroom. Then she screamed for my sister, who just kept reading. When my sister finally arrived, my mom opened the medicine cabinet, grabbed our vitamins, opened the bottle, and emptied it onto the floor.

She screamed, "You are so bad! You can't even take your vitamins like I ask you to! I can't take it! Now clean up this mess. Pick up every single one!"

"I'm sorry!" I wept. "I will take them every day, just like you tell us. I swear!" I screamed back at her. "I swear! I swear!" I yelled louder and louder, but nothing seemed to help.

She walked into the hallway, looking exhausted. She leaned against the wall and slid down till she was sitting on the floor, still crying. My dad peeked halfway up the stairs. He was crying now, too. I had seen my mom cry a lot, but I had never seen my dad cry. I thought I was crying as hard as I possibly could, but seeing him cry made it even worse.

I knelt down on the bathroom floor to help my sister pick up the tiny pink fluoride pills. There were so many I couldn't find a place to kneel where they wouldn't stick into my knees like needles. I thought back to when the long arm was stretching to heaven the first time and wondered what I could have done after that so none of this would be happening.

My dad pulled my mom to her feet and hugged her for a second. Looking out of the corner of my eye, I thought it was over, but then she started punching his chest and screaming, "Don't touch me! Don't touch me!" He tried to hold her close enough that she couldn't punch anymore, but it didn't work. I knew then that she hated him.

I thought he would leave and never come back. A part of me wished he would leave just to save himself from her, but the thought also terrified me. I couldn't imagine being left alone with her. He yelled at me to go to my room, but instead, I ran past them and down the stairs, so I had a place to escape. When I reached the kitchen, I saw my dinner scattered on the floor and my favorite plate smashed in a million pieces, confirming that some of this was indeed my fault. I should have finished eating. I didn't want to go back upstairs but needed to hide in my room. I sat on the bottom stair, listening to the screaming and staring at the front door. I could run through it and escape if they came back down. Finally, I heard only faint sniffling and a door slam shut.

I walked up the stairs slowly, terrified they would burst into the hallway again. When I reached the top, there was silence. I didn't know what had happened while I was gone, but their bedroom door was shut. I slid under my covers and stared through the curtains at the night sky. I imagined that if it got bad enough, I could jump out the window onto the kitchen roof and escape. I couldn't do that in pajamas, so I stayed in my play clothes, which felt weird against the bedsheets. I picked at the corner of the wallpaper near the window's edge, waiting to hear if the yelling would start again, and just when I thought I had no tears left, a few more ran down my cheek. In the silence, I wondered if one of them had left or died, and I didn't know which idea made me feel worse. My eyes felt swollen and burned, but I made them stay wide open for as long as I could while I prayed. The last time I looked at my clock, both arms were reaching for heaven.

The Acorn

THROUGHOUT MY JOURNEY OF HEALING, I meditated a lot on my past experiences. I had no agenda or expectations. I just believed that if I opened up and emptied myself, I would find something—or something would find me. Sometimes I found breadcrumbs leading me further down my path. Sometimes I dropped into moments in my life that were still open wounds, like revisiting a scene in a movie. Sometimes I found myself in the cave I feared most.

This time, I revisited that little girl doing something I remember doing for countless hours at a time, and was given an answer to a question I didn't know I was asking.

The sun pierced through puffy white clouds, illuminating the precious few autumn leaves that remained. They hung off half-bared branches in a last gasp to display their brilliance while a cool, gentle breeze gave them permission to loosen their grip and dance for me.

The rustle of the branches was drowned out only by the crunch of acorns below my feet. As I approached the pebbled driveway, it appeared shorter than I remembered, as did the walkway to the front door. It seemed as though the entire yard had shrunk, while only the trees and I had grown.

Making my way down the driveway, I paused at the back door. I remembered running through it on beautiful summer mornings, bursting to get outside. I also remembered banging my fists on the glass panes on frigid winter evenings as dusk settled in, begging to finally come inside.

I took a deep breath and continued toward the backyard. As I approached, I heard a faint humming. It sounded familiar not only to my ears, but to my heart. I closed my eyes and inhaled slowly as if to breathe the notes into my soul.

Turning the corner, I scanned the yard slowly to take it all in—the treehouse, the sandbox, the jungle gym. It all looked even smaller still, yet exactly the same.

Apprehensively, I turned toward the humming and found her sitting on top of the picnic table. She was completely illuminated by the sun and surrounded by acorns and Dixie cups.

I seemed to have gone unseen. So as not to startle her, I quietly asked, "What are you doing?"

"Collecting treasures," she replied, never looking up.

I walked a little closer and noticed that her work had produced cups full of little baby acorns she was skillfully extracting from their protective caps.

"I have 20 more cups full of them on the shelf in my room," she said.

"Oh, wow! That's a lot. What do you do with them?" I asked.

"I save them," she replied matter-of-factly.

"From what?" I asked, waiting as I watched her work methodically through her pile. I got no response.

She grabbed another acorn, cracked the cap, and peeled back the layers, exposing the treasure underneath it before dropping it safely into another cup.

The Answer: The seed of the mighty oak sleeps within the baby acorn. It holds the oak's essence, the infinite wisdom of the Universe. More power and pure potential than can be appreciated until the oak matures into its destiny.

This little girl, scared and scarred, took that acorn, that essence, that potential, and with love in her heart, built walls around it. She vowed to protect it from failure, abandonment, and isolation, and to save it from the fear and pain she felt and could not process.

Her strength and courage were not enough to save those around her, so she turned inward to save herself. And so, the warrior set out, not knowing that these walls would not protect her from dying; they would prevent her from living her pure potentiality like the oak.

The Question: What was my fascination with baby acorns really all about, and when did I start building the walls that would ultimately imprison me?

Chapter 2

The Tea Set

"Making tea is a ritual that stops the world from falling in on you."
—Jonathan Stroud

THERE WAS A YELLOW PLASTIC shelving unit in the bedroom I shared with my sister. It sat on the floor and soared to the ceiling. The fourth shelf was the highest one I could reach. There I kept my most valuable thing, the bank filled with all the coins I found and earned doing chores; my most precious thing, all of the Dixie cups full of my baby acorns, and my most favorite thing, my tea set.

I didn't spend a lot of time in my room because I was terrified to be on the second floor alone. There were lots of places for bad people and scary things to hide, and no one would hear me screaming for help. The one exception was to have a tea party. I always felt safe with all of my guests sitting at the table and listening to my stories. I imagined places so far away that I forgot all about the bad and the scary.

My house—along with only two other houses—was on a short street adjacent to "The Projects." I didn't exactly know what The Projects meant, given I was only six, but I knew that the boys who started stealing my toys from our yard lived there.

One day, after school, my mom and I walked in the front door and found everything upside down. I didn't understand what was happening.

"Are we moving?" I asked.

She broke down in tears and said that someone broke into our house and stole from us. We found the window they came in, and my eyes landed on the shattered glass all over the floor. The sight of that window changed something inside me.

Despite the chaos that sometimes rained down on my house, it was still my safe place. The one place I knew no one could get to me. I never realized how wrong I had been and how exposed I was to threats I hadn't even imagined yet until I saw the shattered glass on the floor. I looked around the house and saw all the other windows in a whole new way. They used to be pictures of the beautiful outside world. Now, they were opportunities for anyone with a rock or a bat to climb into my house and steal anything they wanted, even me.

I ran to my room, wondering if they had made it that far. There wasn't a mess like I had found on the first floor, but I saw dirt on the floor and knew someone had been there. I scanned the fourth shelf first, relieved to find my bank still there and all my Dixie cups lined up perfectly.

Then I noticed something *was* missing. I looked over the room to see if I had left it out or if they had just moved it, but to my horror, it was nowhere to be found. I felt sick to my stomach and started to shake.

My tea set was gone.

That tea set was often the doorway to my greatest escapes. My dolls and stuffed animals surrounded me, sipping invisible tea and listening attentively to my stories. I took them on adventures and made sure they were safe. Now it was gone, and I was devastated. What would I tell them? How could they feel safe now if I couldn't protect the tea set?

My shoulders dropped as if my hands were holding 40-pound bags of pain. My head tilted back, opening the airway to my soul, and I let out a visceral wail. Tears rushed from the corners of my clenched lids, drenching my face. I was drowning in my loss. It was all I had … my only escape, and it was gone.

Hearing this, my mother rushed to my room screaming, "What?! What?!"

"Why not take my bank and buy whatever you want? Why take my tea set?!" I repeated the sentence over and over. I couldn't imagine that they could see the magic of my tea set just by looking at it on my shelf—I couldn't make sense of it.

I assumed it was the same boys who stole my outside toys and asked if I could walk to The Projects with my bank and propose a trade. I would gladly give up every cent I had for the tea set I knew was irreplaceable. My mother explained that while a generous idea, it was not a particularly safe one for a 6-year-old girl. When she refused to go in my place, I became even more hysterical.

In the past, I felt unsafe in my own home, but I knew those monsters. I knew what would trigger the yelling and crying. And I knew how to help prevent it from happening or where to hide when it did. Now, I had a new enemy, something on the outside of my house. This one was faceless, unpredictable, and completely out of my control. And I thought about it constantly.

A few months later, we moved to a new house in a new town that my parents thought was safer. Unfortunately, I didn't leave my fears behind like I did those boys. I packed them up and took them with me. Now the first floor was scarier than the second, and that is exactly where my new bedroom was … the first floor.

Most nights, I lay awake listening for even the slightest noise of someone lurking outside my house looking for a window to break. I sealed the window shade tight to the glass, knowing that it could not protect me from those dangers, only hide them from me. Still, I struggled to stay awake and remain vigilant, convinced that the moment I fell asleep, the invasion would begin.

On other nights I didn't seal the shade. Instead, I peeked through the crack at the night sky. The stars reminded me of how small and insignificant I was. I started thinking about my own death and wondered if anyone would notice I was gone. The Universe seemed too big to notice the loss of a girl who'd only just turned seven. Then I graduated to contemplating where I would go once I died and where I was before I was born. Those questions were new, and they terrified me. Once they settled in, I wished I could go back to before I ever asked them.

I talked to God about purgatory and heaven. And then there was hell, which the nuns made very clear was a distinct possibility, even for me. I asked God where I was before I was born. Where *was* I?! I was nowhere because *I* didn't exist. That must be where I was going back to when I died… a black hole of nothingness. My heart pounded and my hands clutched the corners of my blanket. I clenched my eyes shut only to find the black void that I feared as the tears ran down my face. I prayed for answers, but most of all, I prayed for distractions from the never-ending and increasingly paralyzing thoughts swirling through my mind. And closing my eyes only reminded me of the nothingness, so there was nowhere to hide.

The night sky, the noises, and even the silence triggered thoughts I couldn't run from. It was during this time that the world inside me became just as scary as the world around me. My thoughts were no longer within my control. They could turn on me and become my worst enemy.

This was the birth of my anxiety. On the nights that it overwhelmed me, I would steal away to my parents' room on the second floor. On a good night, I would find my father in the middle of their queen bed, slip onto the edge, and close my eyes, hoping to fall asleep before he rolled over. When he eventually did roll over, I usually did too ... right onto the floor.

There was no cuddling, though. If he found me there, he would send me back to bed. If Mom found me, there would be hell to pay. So, my only hope was to stay silent and invisible. On most nights, I curled up on the floor on my father's side of the bed and fell asleep shivering. No matter how cold I got, it was still better than being on the first floor. And I was so focused on my father's every breath and shift that it provided exactly the distraction I needed to quiet my mind and finally fall asleep.

Chapter 3

The Scary Thoughts

"Worry is a misuse of the imagination."
—Dan Zadra

WHEN WE MOVED to the new town, it seemed like my parents' top priority was finding a new Chinese take-out restaurant—even before unpacking all the boxes. The first night we tried it, I had my first panic attack. My parents attributed my symptoms to too much MSG because when they asked what was wrong, I had no answer. I wasn't hiding anything yet; I just honestly didn't know.

My father took me outside on that bone-chilling winter night, and we walked around the block until it ended. We stood under each streetlight and held our breath together for five seconds. When we finally exhaled, the light from above lit up the water crystals, making it look like I was breathing fire.

This was when my imagination started to turn on me. The tea parties were the last time I trusted my mind not to go to scary places. After that, awful thoughts crept in more and more, and it became harder and harder to protect myself from them.

I didn't tell anyone about my scary thoughts because I didn't want them to get mad or think I wasn't brave or normal. But there were certain times when my panic was too much to hide. The first place was in church. We went every Sunday. We usually sat in the front, and the five of us took up an entire pew.

Unlike most kids, I loved church. I had a very close relationship with God, Mary, and Jesus. They knew me better than my real family because I couldn't hide anything from them. They knew all my scary thoughts and loved me anyway. They protected me all day and stayed with me all night until I fell asleep. I thought church was the safest place in the world. That is, until something changed inside of me that I didn't understand.

One Sunday, just after the second reading, my heart started racing like after the Chinese food. I didn't know why, but just sitting in the pew was scaring me. I didn't feel afraid of anything in particular, I just felt like I had to escape. The more I saw barriers between me and the door, the more I panicked. I would get in trouble if I talked during the readings, never mind asking to leave in the middle of the service and making a scene. Those thoughts made me feel even more trapped.

That's when I started dreading church. Months went by until one Sunday, I said I didn't want to go. When my parents asked why, I finally told them what was happening. They let me sit at the end of the pew after that. I glanced back at the door constantly and yawned repeatedly to catch my breath. Sometimes I left to go to the bathroom during "pass the peace" when there was enough commotion that no one could see me. I didn't actually use the toilet; I just went to breathe.

I'd feel like it was over, but just a few minutes after returning to my pew, I'd be gasping for air again. I stopped going to communion because my legs felt too weak to stand. I prayed for it to go away as hard as I could, but it never did. I reasoned that it was probably because there were so many other people in church praying at the same time, and God had a hard time hearing me.

Then I became scared of water. My mother's explanation was a toilet overflowing, which I didn't remember. No one could really understand it because they couldn't see what I saw inside my mind— the water filling the house or car, the hands on the windows grasping at life, the corpses floating on the water. I don't have a first memory of rain, the toilet, or a carwash. I only remember believing that every one of them would lead me to a watery grave.

One Saturday afternoon, on a family drive, I watched the rain fall from the backseat and tried counting the drops to distract myself. It worked at first, and then they started falling too fast. I looked at each face in the car to see if they were as scared as me. No one seemed to even notice the rain. They didn't see the danger like I did. I watched the cars around us as the visibility faded and the water sprayed off the road. My entire body shook, and my tears fell as fast as the rain. I became hysterical and screamed to pull over. If we were on a highway, my parents would stop under a bridge until the rain subsided. But this time, we were in the middle of a town I didn't recognize.

My father took a left turn down a hill to park in the lot behind a Friendly's. I watched in horror as the water rushed past our car in waves, flooding the flat road below us. I knew the water would eventually reach our car and drown us all. When they tried to distract me with Donna Summer, I realized that none of them fully appreciated the assault we were under. We were sitting in a coffin waiting to die. The rain grew louder and louder on the roof of the car. I put my hands over my ears, closed my eyes as tight as I could, and wailed with every exhale. I was always convinced that once it started, it wouldn't stop.

The car wash was no different. It was just a coffin inside another coffin. This was especially difficult to control when I was in a friend's car. They acted like my family and weren't afraid of rain or car washes. My best friend's family actually went to the car wash *for fun*! I waited outside and ate my donut alone. My best friend's sister made fun of me. I thought it made me smart and brave.

When my panic started to spread into time with my friends, I started making excuses and lying to hide it. It was especially bad when I agreed to sleep at their house. Most kids call their parents to pick them up at a friend's house during a sleepover at one time or another. They get scared in a strange house or get into a fight with their friend. But I stopped having sleepovers—even in my own house. Having someone in my room all night and not being able to change my mind and send them home made me panic. I needed things a certain way to calm my mind, and a friend sleeping in my room created some chaos in my mind, some sense of disorder.

This need for order and control to feel safe became obsessive and compulsive in my house after sunset. I knew that most of the chaos in my house happened after dark, and I could only handle one chaotic situation at a time. I needed to make certain that everything else was in order—all doors and windows closed and locked, no screens, even in the hellish heat of summer. No dishes in the sink, no magazines out of order, no showers to be taken. Everyone and everything in its place by sundown, no exceptions. I didn't always get my way, so I panicked until the exhaustion finally took over and I fell asleep.

Over time, I was convinced the adults just weren't qualified to keep me safe. I started identifying risks and doing the worrying for them. I was afraid of more things than any other kids I knew, but I wasn't afraid of the panic attacks yet. If the adults would just let me control things, I wouldn't have to panic at all.

My biggest fears remained the scary thoughts, and I remember the first time they came and didn't leave. I was in the fifth grade when that fog settled in. I felt trapped and alone with them in some place that felt separate from my own life somehow, and it lasted for months. The more I focused on the thoughts, the thicker the fog got—and the further away I slipped. It's clear to me now that I was suffering from an undiagnosed depressive episode with some characteristics of dissociation.

It was the thoughts about death that I'd only had at night that were now following me around all day. Dying was the scariest thing I could think of, so then I wondered if I could cause it. Could I hurt myself and die? Then I wondered if I could hurt someone else. These thoughts terrified me because I couldn't imagine hurting anyone. I considered asking my parents to remove the knives from our house but knew they would think I was crazy. And I couldn't blame them. I knew I wasn't bad, so maybe I was crazy.

I finally found my way out of that fog by creating a box in my mind. I took all those thoughts, put them in it, and closed it tight. Then I pushed the box as far back in my mind as I could. I didn't know how long it would last, but the fog finally lifted, and I felt safe.

Until something opened it back up again.

Chapter 4

The Pretty One

"Pretty is not the rent you pay to exist in the world as a woman."
—Unknown

I WATCHED MY MOTHER battle her weight since my first memory of her. I heard the word "thighs" used in a negative way so often that to this day, the sound of it makes me sick to my stomach. It's like mucus or puberty—no redeeming quality for the ear or the mind.

At home, I watched her count calories and weigh her food on a small food scale in our linoleum-laden kitchen. At Workout World, I sat patiently in the babysitting room. As a 10-year-old, I felt almost old enough to be the babysitter. I scanned the room for her green leotard and leg warmers in a sea of women jumping, kicking, and waving their hands in the air to disco beats.

As I stood behind the baby gate with arms crossed, I was forming opinions of those women, my mother, and ultimately about myself that would last decades. I didn't see empowerment and positive body image. I saw women checking boxes on their progress charts. I saw skinny instructors clapping with encouraging smiles. Most of all, I saw leotards full of shame. Women judging and comparing themselves to each other. I saw battle lines drawn between thin and fat. I digested my mother's comments on the ride home about who had gained and who had lost. Losing was winning, and gaining was losing. It was that simple, yet that confusing.

Covering the walls of Workout World were posters of emaciated models projecting an "ideal" that didn't inspire as much as taunt these women screaming, "Don't you wish you were me?" Ultimately, I learned that my mother never felt good enough because of the size of her thighs and the number on a scale.

Heading into middle school, I outgrew the babysitting room, and my mother outgrew Workout World. She and my father started daily workouts in our living room early in the morning, while I ate pancakes and watched from the kitchen. Gilad from *Bodies in Motion* and the *20 Minute Workout* girls became like part of the family. While I'm grateful for the awareness of physical fitness that it instilled in me, at the time, I simply saw it as my parents beating back the tireless tide of weight gain and negative self-image.

Unfortunately, I loved to eat. Food was my friend. It was a delicious and much-needed distraction from the time I woke till the minute I went to bed—and sometimes in the middle of the night. Smelling food cooking in the kitchen comforted me and made me feel safe. And when my mind started reaching for those thoughts locked away in the box, I reached for the refrigerator and refocused my attention on the buffet inside.

Then I found my thighs. It was a Sunday, and I'd just finished peeling a large bag of potatoes. We always ate roast beef and mashed potatoes on football Sundays. I was sitting in a wingback chair in the corner of our living room, marveling at my accomplishment and smelling the aroma of roast beef wafting from the oven.

When I placed the pot of peeled potatoes on the floor, I glanced down at my thighs. For the first time in my life, they looked big. While everyone was engrossed in the game, I was suddenly engrossed in the size of my legs. *When did this happen? How could it have gone unnoticed? Is it these corduroys?* I thought, shame coursing through my veins. I was only 12 years old.

For the next 30 years, I placed a pillow or a coat on my lap to muffle the sound of my thighs screaming at me. And I never had that warm, safe feeling when I smelled roast beef again, either. That smell suddenly carried consequences. And the first time I heard that a boy liked me, I thought, *How is that possible with these thighs?*

Report cards came out that next Wednesday. Normally this would have been my sole focus being a vigilant student, but that week I was too busy comparing my thighs, my breasts, my arms, and every other body part to my peers.

At dinner that night, my father reviewed my grades, looked up, and said, "Well, you'll never be the pretty one." Then he scanned the table for nods of agreement. I looked around the table, too, only to see blank stares.

"What? It's not a bad thing. You'll just have to make up for it in other ways, and good grades are a great place to start. Keep it up," he continued, as if patting himself on the back for giving me a compliment.

I thought bringing home straight A's would have elicited a different response. *Maybe I was the last one to notice my thighs*, I thought. But his comment reached well beyond my thighs, which made me wonder what else was I missing. I nodded my head in agreement, cleared my plate, and went straight to my room.

Standing in front of my bureau, I looked at myself in the mirror and wondered what he saw. This wasn't the first time I looked at myself critically. I was in the eighth grade now and saw the attention certain girls were getting from the boys. I knew what was "pretty" and what was not. But I didn't think there was anything particularly wrong with me beyond my thighs, nor did I think what I looked like at 12 years old would define how I looked forever... until now, maybe.

I saw a nose that had grown too big for my face and ears that stuck out from my hair. My Greek grandfather told me that they both grew bigger every day of your life until you die. Looking at his nose and ears, that terrified me. If that were true, I could see my father's point.

I also saw a forehead that my grandfather insisted required bangs and lips that drew racial slurs from the neighborhood kids. Then there was the gaping space between my front teeth. I was suddenly hideous and powerless to change any of it.

I laid face down on my bed, soaking the pillowcase with tears. I felt hurt and ashamed. If my own father didn't think I was pretty, no one would.

In that moment, I was transported back to lying on my stomach in the secret lower level of my neighbor's fort. It was the summer before, and they were looking at a Playboy centerfold. It was the first time I'd seen an image like that.

My neighbors were all boys who were slightly older than me. This fort was in the backyard of two brothers. We would hang out in there or hide during a game of kick the can. The lower level was only about three feet high, so we had to slide in on our bellies. I don't remember how we all ended up there that day, or exactly what they said as we looked at images of these naked women, but I do remember how their comments made me feel.

I was initially horrified that someone had taken photos of these poor women while they were naked, convinced it had been done against their will. The shame of it overwhelmed me. Then I remember being even more horrified at how excited the boys acted as they pointed at different body parts and discussed size, shape, and color.

I quietly slid myself backward on my stomach and exited the fort feet-first. No one noticed. I heard a collective gasp as another page turned. I paused, dusted some dirt off my pants, and zipped my sweatshirt up to my neck. It wasn't cold out, but those images and comments had a chilling effect on me. I never went back to the fort again.

I requested a new bathing suit that summer, too—one with a lot of material. The more coverage, the better. I stopped floating on my dad's back around the pool. I stopped kissing my parents goodnight. I watched men at the public pool look at women and girls and wondered if they were thinking all the same things that the boys had said that day.

Back at school, boys started making similar comments. The pretty girls were complimented and idolized, not-so-pretty girls were ignored or teased, and the fast-developing girls were jeered and ridiculed.

Now, lying on that bed as a 12-year-old, I realized that my body was not my own. It was something to be objectified, judged, and sexualized by others without my permission. Whether it was the women in Workout World, the boys in the fort, or my own father, I was now being labeled by my size, shape, and color. It was how the world would form its opinion of me before I ever opened my mouth. And my father knew it.

I struggled with what this all meant. If getting straight A's was a great way to overcome my disappointing looks, did that mean if I was pretty, I didn't need good grades? Was being the pretty one the goal? Was being a good student somehow plan B because plan A wasn't working out? If I wasn't going to be the pretty one, I would be the smart one. OK, but he said, "make up for it in other ways." That sounded like I was defective. I knew that being pretty would get me the boys' attention, but beyond that, I didn't see what it had to do with my grades.

The summer after eighth grade, I went on my first diet to prepare for all the new kids in high school who hadn't seen my thighs yet. I was determined to prove my father wrong and get on the right side of this judgment and jeering. And I believed that if I looked good enough, then my grades would actually matter. People would care about what was on the inside, not just the outside. I saw how the less attractive, smart girls were categorized and dismissed, so I needed to pass this test.

My mother and I joined Weight Watchers and counted calories together. Each day, I woke up and ate "diet" toast with sugar-free jam for breakfast, then walked three miles with my mother before we ate salads with dry tuna fish and pita bread for lunch. I even stopped seeing friends and watching TV with my family at night so I could be in bed early and not snack after dinner. I drank 24 Dixie cups of tap water a day and logged my progress on the refrigerator door. I lost 10 pounds that summer.

Initially, I referred to fashion magazines for inspiration, and soon became completely smitten with them. I devoured every page, knew every model's name, and could identify photographers and designers with just one glance. I loved the art, the freedom of expression, and the photography. But at that time, there were no models over a certain age or weight. Waifs who looked too skinny to stand were fashion house muses and marketed as the ideal body type. This imagery was not only unrealistic but unhealthy, and I consumed it like an addict. When I looked up from the pages and saw my mother's thighs, her self-loathing suddenly made sense.

It was now clear that my physical appearance was paramount. Being perfect in athletics and academics was not going to be enough. The boys across the street were not lying in the fort looking at girls' report cards. Similarly, I was not looking at magazines with pictures of female athletes to form my body image because none existed. The vast majority of women in *Sports Illustrated* were in string bikinis lying at the wave break, not in uniforms taking a water break.

This was not a box of my own choosing, but a box society was force-fitting me into because I was female. I was handed this burden of pursuing an ideal I didn't get to vote on—a perfectionism that promoted looking like someone other than myself—and it planted the seeds of eating disorders and constant comparison that reinforced my self-loathing and exacerbated my anxiety.

I would gain back the 10 pounds I lost on that first diet over and over again until, ultimately, I was 60 pounds heavier. For years, whenever I finally reached my goal weight, a flood of anxiety washed over me, stealing any pleasure I thought that number would bring. I panicked at the thought of eating even a morsel of food, convinced I would gain it all back. And I was right. When I finally did eat, I didn't stop until I had gained everything back and more. The journey back up was full of anxiety, too, wondering, *When am I going to stop? What if I can't lose it again? Why am I so out of control?* The irony is that eating was what made me feel better temporarily when those scary thoughts surfaced. My only peace was in the struggle. Focusing on a goal kept my mind occupied. I felt in control, which reduced my anxiety. But I was never happy where I was. I let my mind control my food intake rather than learning how to control my mind and let the intake naturally follow.

At its worst, this hyper-focus on body image convinced me that I was replaceable. Regardless of my grades, my accomplishments, my thoughts, or my beliefs, my physical appearance would always be the most important factor.

When those boys unknowingly lured me into this competition, they failed to tell me it was un-winnable. Even if I played and became the pretty one, they would always turn the page.

Chapter 5

The Trophy

*"It's the possibility of having a dream come true
that makes life interesting."*
—Paolo Coelho

THE MICROPHONE CRACKLED as the emcee said, "Now, we will present the trophy to the most valuable eighth-grade girl basketball player in town. Coach, please come to the podium to announce your winner of this prestigious award." I can still feel the curve of the wooden auditorium seat beneath me as my body tingled with anticipation.

Two years earlier, I had set my sights on the biggest prize in town—at least if you were playing youth basketball. It was a trophy that towered over three feet tall and was awarded to the best boy and girl basketball player at what felt like the biggest award ceremony ever held.

The rumors surrounding who was in the running for such an honor began in the seventh grade. There were whispers in the stands and private conversations among the parents and coaches. I played every game with that trophy in the back of my mind. As the seventh-grade season progressed, I could see other girls on my team progressing, too, especially on offense. I had always shied away from offense because there were so many opportunities to fail. Dribbling and shooting only exposed weaknesses, and I wanted no part of it.

Defense was my sweet spot—my safe place. It was about determination and heart, hard work and hustle. And I was willing to bleed on that court to be the best defender in town. But at some point, I realized that was not going to be enough.

So, in the dead of winter, I started waking up an hour early to do ball-handling drills. When my alarm went off, I pulled a sweatshirt on over my pajamas, tied my sneakers, and stumbled through a dark house half awake. I tugged on the string hanging from the ceiling to turn on the single light bulb that illuminated a small corner of the unheated garage. I pressed play on my tape deck and started my stopwatch. I drilled and drilled and drilled. Then I jumped rope with still heavy eyelids closing on me. Then I drilled some more until it was time to get ready for school.

After school, I played in the street, always adjusting for the warped particle board that was my backboard and the fact that our street was on a hill. When the sun set, I retreated into our basement to lift weights that my dad had bought 20 years earlier. The ceiling was too low for jumping rope, so line jumps and foot fire closed out the night. There were no days off. I needed to be fully armed with as many offensive weapons as possible when I stepped out on that court. I applied the same drive and determination I had on defense to fine-tune my new skills. The garage, the basement, and the street became my armory. I spent the next six years on that regimen.

Winning that trophy was the proudest moment of my life at the time. I felt invincible. If only I knew then that my discipline and drive would be my superpower. I had hustle and willpower to spare, and now I had confidence, too, in both my mental and physical abilities.

That award also gave me a distinction going into high school, as well as something to defend. I needed to prove I was worthy of it. So, the hours in the gym expanded even after long practices. The harder I worked, the better I got. The results fueled more motivation, and it became a virtuous cycle.

The anxiety seemed dormant during this time. I was excelling in school and had enough homework to keep my mind occupied when I wasn't thinking about friends, boyfriends, and the next big game. Everything was in its place, there was less chaos at home, and there seemed to be order in my world. I was thriving. And I was working so hard all day that there was no lying up at night contemplating my angst. I was exhausted and fell asleep the minute my head hit the pillow. I had become disciplined at never speaking of or looking directly at the box where my scary thoughts were locked away.

In my eyes, my future was very clear. I had short-term plans to ace a test on Tuesday, play my best game of the year on Thursday, and wear my boyfriend's football jersey to school on Friday before heading to the big game with my friends on Saturday. And I had long-term plans to ace the SATs, land a scholarship to an Ivy League college, and play basketball until I graduated and went to law school. With hard work and focus, doors would open, and my life would unfold in obvious and amazing ways. I was on top of the world and confident it was only getting better.

But my long-term goals didn't quite materialize the way I had foreseen. As I'd hoped, colleges were recruiting me for basketball. What I hadn't expected was that the track coach at Dartmouth College would see me throw the javelin at the State Finals my junior year and start recruiting me as well.

As you can imagine, throwing the javelin was something I stumbled into and, strangely enough, excelled at. It was not my favorite sport, just arguably my best sport at the time. It was certainly not something I thought I could parlay into an Ivy League education.

I remember only two things from those first conversations with the coach—he would not allow me to play two sports, and he strongly suggested I apply for early decision. *What are the chances?* I thought. *When I don't get in, I will just continue to pursue basketball as planned.* It was only one college application, and the thrill of even applying to an Ivy League school intoxicated me. Then the letter arrived.

It was mid-December, and I was deep into basketball practices for my senior year as team captain. There were high expectations of winning States, and a heavy weight on my shoulders. I planned to eat, study, and fall asleep exhausted, just as I did every weeknight. It was well after dark when I arrived home, sweaty and exhausted.

When I walked through the front door, I found streamers hanging from the cabinets and the letter lying open on the kitchen table. My parents looked overjoyed. They had opened the envelope before I even arrived. Only one person in my town had ever gone to an Ivy League school, so this was a big event.

Unfortunately, the only thing on my mind was basketball. I had never considered this would actually happen. I couldn't comprehend giving up everything I had worked so hard for. I couldn't imagine this season being my last. I broke down in tears.

"I'm not going!" I screamed. My parents were shocked at my reaction. It was an Ivy League school, after all.

Crying uncontrollably, I grabbed the letter and my car keys and stormed out the door. I drove 40 minutes to a nearby college where I had attended basketball camp every summer since I was 10 years old. I had become friends with a basketball star there. He was my mentor, and I needed his counsel.

I told him what had happened as the tears continued to flow. I wouldn't let him get a word in until he finally yelled, with a big smile, "Just sit down and listen!"

"Your life's work is not to play basketball. The lessons you have learned through basketball, both on and off the court, are *life lessons*. Teamwork, leadership, determination, mental toughness. Now is the time to take those lessons and translate them into your life."

Bullshit! I thought. Intellectually, I knew he was right, but I wasn't ready to internalize it yet. I always knew my time with basketball would serve a bigger purpose in my life. But that did not make my decision easier. I struggled for weeks afterward. I knew it was a foregone conclusion that I could not turn down an Ivy League school and would have to face the reality of losing basketball forever. But I still vacillated until the very last minute.

Ultimately, I made the excruciating choice and took the terrifying road less traveled. I could have followed my teammates and played basketball at a local college. I had full scholarships, which meant no student debt or working every day after track practice. But I sacrificed my passion and comfort, both mentally and financially, for something that I thought would offer me more. I'm sure some people go to college excited about leaving high school behind and making a new impression and a fresh start. But leaving basketball behind was the hardest thing I had ever done.

What seemed like the logical, best choice for me at the time pulled a small thread in my psyche that started an unraveling. I didn't just leave the basketball court. I left my identity—my safe place, my confidence, my people. Over those six years, I had created a life that I thrived in. I had support systems in place with my friends, family, neighbors, teammates, coaches, teachers, principals, and counselors. I had routines that kept me physically and mentally fit. My confidence and determination were overshadowing any doubts or anxieties that bubbled to the surface. I was in the zone, a sweet spot—socially, academically, and athletically—where the stars aligned and, on most days, where nothing held me back. The harder I worked, the more I achieved. I was on top of the world.

It yielded an opportunity to reach a level I had only dreamed of. But it required the greatest sacrifice. Walking away from it all—all that I created, all that I knew and loved—all that protected me from the box in the back of my mind. It would require me to burn it all to the ground and completely start over. And I'd have to keep that box shut long enough just to survive.

Part 2

LIVING IN THE BOX

Chapter 6

What No One Sees

*"Anxiety is a thin stream of fear trickling through the mind.
If encouraged, it cuts a channel into which all other
thoughts are drained."*
—Arthur Somers Roche

MOMENTS STRUNG TOGETHER become days that add up to weeks and
sometimes months that feel normal. You don't dare wonder why or
analyze. You just avoid and try to forget, knowing it could find its
way back in at any moment, and it can all come crashing down again.
You don't really know how to keep it in the box, so you constantly
try to outrun it.

But it's like caging a wild animal. In the quiet moments, you are
haunted by the sound of its feet shuffling slowly across the floor as
it circles its cage. In the background, you feel its rage building over
time the longer it feels contained and confined. It waits for a moment

of weakness when the caretaker's vigilance falters, and she leaves the door open just slightly or forgets that she left it unlocked. An innocent question, a passing thought, a memory, an unwelcome trigger, and the door slides open just enough to expose your greatest fear. The wave comes rushing back in, crashing over you.

Now the animal circles *you* in the same pattern it walked while caged, and in an instant, the roles are reversed, and you are the prisoner again.

The attack comes quickly, with little warning, and has a clear beginning, middle, and end. At best, you diffuse it. At worst, you feel like you will surely die. Something has stolen your breath and cinched your chest. Your mind races through the scenarios—how long can I last without oxygen, is there a blood clot, am I having a stroke? Then the warm wave of terror washes over your body, making every hair stand on the end of a million goosebumps.

The immediate shot of adrenaline is so intense it feels like fire running through your veins. Your heart pounds, and then in one beat, free falls into your abdomen, causing another desperate gasp for air as you reach for your neck to take your pulse. Your hands shake, causing more panic as you are convinced your heart will surely stop if you are not counting and confirming each beat.

Just when you think your heart is beating so hard it will burst from your chest, you get out of the car, leave the restaurant or church or play or concert, find juice or beer or wine, take a deep breath … and find a way out. You live to see another day, another sunrise and sunset, and likely another panic attack.

Then there is the generalized anxiety that starts with the fear of nothing and everything and expands with the fear of more panic attacks. It settles into your bones and becomes a part of you like a parasite finding a host, depressing you deeper into a thick fog. There is no specific threat, only scary thoughts, a sense of dread, disconnection, loss, and nothingness. There is no beginning, middle, or end.

You wake with a dull headache that lasts all day. Your jaw is clenched, and your breath is shallow. The bones in your face pound and your teeth throb to the rhythm of your heartbeat. Your arms and legs are weak like rubber bands. Passing dizzy spells simmer into a constant curse. Acid builds in your stomach and burns a hole through it each day.

If you suffer long enough, depersonalization and derealization give your mind a break from the overload, and this is when you are convinced you have gone crazy. You feel as if something has taken over your body, and you are just an observer watching it move you around and give you words to say—like reading a script devoid of opinion or expression. Everything you see on the outside of you, even your own body, feels distant. You feel locked in a clear bubble that makes everything numb.

No one notices the change except those who really know you. They tilt their head and look deep into your lifeless eyes and ask, "What is *wrong* with you?"

A voice in your head screams, "I DON'T KNOW! PLEASE HELP ME!" But what slides out of your mouth sounds more like "Nothing. Why?"

You can't describe it or explain it, and have no idea how to ask for help.

You wake up with no recollection of yesterday, no plans for today, and no interest in tomorrow. There is just a void—no emotions attached to your thoughts or actions, no anticipation or excitement, no happiness or joy, no sadness or fear except the trace of terror underlying your awareness that this is happening. Where *am* I? The reflection in the mirror is not particularly familiar. Your face is expressionless, and your eyes are empty. When the fog finally lifts, the fear that it will return is terrifying.

Weeks go by, months are lost, therapists are concerned, families are confused, friends are patient, relationships are broken, and with every ounce of courage you can find, you move through the fog deliberately, inch by inch, desperately hoping that eventually, the light will overtake it.

Chapter 7

The Identity Crisis

"I do not at all understand the mystery of grace—
only that it meets us where we are
but does not leave us where it found us."
—Anne Lamott

I SAT ON THE EDGE OF MY BED PARALYZED, holding the phone in one hand and the scrap of paper I'd scribbled the number on in the other. The window shades were tightly drawn, keeping the mid-afternoon sunlight from entering the room. I was as scared as I could ever remember, terrified at how many times I thought of killing myself in the last two months.

Dying was actually my biggest fear, but my mind had become such a chaotic black hole that it seemed the only way out. I felt completely empty inside, and at the same time, full of something dark and heavy. I recalled a similar darkness that blanketed my life for months in the fifth grade, but I had never felt this kind of depression before. I was looking up from the bottom of a well, sinking deeper each day.

That fall, I had been assigned to a two-story concrete building that was a few blocks from campus. It should have come with mandatory therapy sessions. It was dark and institutional, like a mental health facility. Everything about it made me feel completely disconnected and disturbingly disoriented. The only person I knew there was my roommate.

It was the first quarter of my sophomore year, and I was still struggling. Socially, I was finding it difficult to fit in. Everyone came from better schools and families, and they had expensive clothes and cars. I attended socials at fraternities where boys made fun of my hair and accent.

Academically, I was on probation after a difficult first year. I was behind the minute the bell rang as I was forced to retake advanced placement classes because my high school lacked the proper accreditation. Even with good study habits, I was struggling to keep up, and my grades reflected it. Dartmouth taught things differently than Methuen High School. I had not been trained to write papers and debate in class the way my private and prep school peers had.

Athletically, I was still grieving my loss of basketball and trying to figure out who I was without it. My freshman year didn't reveal me as a sudden track standout. I had plenty of competition. I was also forced to throw the 35-pound weight for the winter season and the hammer for the spring season. The 30 pounds I gained helped those efforts but contributed to my mental slide. I went from a big, beautiful fish flourishing in a small pond to an insignificant, ugly guppy drowning in a big, prestigious ocean.

Who was I now? What did my peers see me as? What was I really doing here? Could I be who I was at home, or did I need to redefine myself? What parts of me would I have to compromise to do that?

What parts did I actually want to grow and evolve versus change just to fit in? I was so grounded in high school. I knew exactly who I was there and where I was going. But no one here knew that person, and even my memory of her was fading.

I dialed the number on my phone, watching my hands shake. When the woman on the other end answered and introduced herself, I froze. Nothing came out of my mouth. The moment was too surreal to step into fully. It was like watching a movie where a girl calls a suicide hotline, and I had no idea what would happen next.

"How can I help you?" she asked, over and over again.

I had no idea how she could help me, so I hung up the phone. I watched it slip out of my hand and onto the floor. I hung my head and wept. I didn't know who *I was* anymore. I was unrecognizable to myself and everyone around me. How had I veered so far off of that path?

Then I heard a whisper: "I wanted to be an inspiration." It reminded me of the previous winter when I had fallen hard for a guy in my class with movie-star good looks—dark, wavy hair, broad shoulders and brooding eyes that nearly disappeared when he smiled. We only had a handful of conversations, the most memorable of which was in his dorm room one night that lasted into the morning hours.

It started awkwardly because we had never been entirely alone together before. But once we sat down in separate chairs on opposite sides of the room and started talking, it felt exciting and comfortable and everything in between.

"So, why are you here? What do you want to do with an *Ivy League* diploma?" he asked, almost making fun of it. Part of his charm was his James Dean, this-place-doesn't-impress-me attitude.

I stared at the lampshade next to his head because I felt incredibly vulnerable looking in his eyes, like he could see right into my soul.

I thought about Abraham Lincoln and Martin Luther King and my obsession with social justice and becoming a lawyer and running for political office. Then I pictured him laughing at all of that and completely dismissing it as "predictable."

So, what *was* behind those obsessions and choices? What was the deeper reason I sacrificed so much to come to Dartmouth? Why did I want to be a lawyer and a politician? What was my real motivation?

"I want to inspire people. I want to lead the sort of life that others will look at and be inspired by, so they can strive for things they never thought possible, so they can believe the unbelievable, so they can live the life they've always dreamed of. I want to fight for those who can't fight for themselves. I want to create those opportunities for them and remove the barriers in their way—no matter who they are or what that means for them."

I was still staring at the lampshade. When I finally peeked back at his face, it was mysteriously expressionless.

What have I done? I thought. *Did that sound so ridiculously naïve and altruistic that I just ruined my chances with this guy?* I had never considered a witty or sexy response. I thought he was looking for an actual answer. But then I thought about what I'd said and felt completely comfortable with it, confident it came directly from my heart and expressed exactly why I was there. Fuck it.

"Maybe that's more general than you were expecting, but yeah, I want to be an inspiration. And you? Why are you here? What do you want to do with all of this?" I asked.

"I just want to play hockey," he replied.

I sat silently with those words hanging in the space between us. What a luxury. I felt far more responsibility than that. My Sunday School teachers always said, "To those who are given much, much is expected." Sitting in his dorm room, I felt the weight of those words for the first time. If I was only the second person from my town to get into an Ivy League school, I was expected to do much with all of this. I wasn't entirely sure what that would look like yet, but I certainly felt the intense pressure of it. While my peers seemed to glide through freshman year, protected by privilege, I was being crushed under the moral obligation of the privilege I had been handed so suddenly by attending this school.

Back on the edge of my bed, staring at the phone on the floor, it was difficult to think about that night now. How would I ever inspire someone if I could completely lose control of my mind? I couldn't remember where I was supposed to be that afternoon—work, track practice, or studying for tests I didn't know were looming? I knew I was meeting friends for dinner but couldn't remember who exactly was coming or what was appropriate to wear. Not for the occasion because there was no occasion. But rather, what did *I* wear? My mind was completely blank.

How could I live up to the responsibility and opportunity I had been given if I had lost myself and, consequently, the ability to find myself again? My worst nightmare was not living up to my potential or the expectations others had for me, and here I was, unable to wake up. I was terrified and exhausted.

But behind it all was a faint whisper, one that would stay with me for years and become a close friend. A whisper telling me to just stand up—just move. Find a place in the sun, sit and see what happens next. And that's exactly what I did. Without the physical capacity or mental resolve, I watched my body rise up off the bed, walk out the door, and find a bench in the sun. That was sometimes how it worked. Grace pulled me from the shadows and into the light.

The following quarter I was scheduled to take my sophomore trip abroad to Mexico. The thought of being in yet another foreign place, living with a family I didn't know, speaking a language I could barely understand—it didn't excite me; it paralyzed me. I thought I was losing my mind and was convinced that living in a foreign country with strangers would only make it worse. I didn't trust myself anymore and was terrified by my loss of control. What was I capable of? Intrusive thoughts about how deeply I could devolve became a vicious and compulsive pastime. What if I went completely crazy and killed everyone in the house and ended up in a Mexican prison for the rest of my life?

I couldn't expose myself or others to the terrifying conclusions I came to, so I devised a plan to abort my time abroad entirely. I called my father from a payphone one afternoon and convinced him that joining a sorority was my first priority. Since we couldn't afford both the initiation dues and the travel expenses, I needed to cancel my trip to Mexico.

Instead, I told him I would return home for the winter quarter and rush the sorority when I was back on campus in the spring. He had strong reservations and asked a lot of questions, but I was adamant. I didn't have the vocabulary to describe how unstable I felt, so I danced around the edges, telling him I just needed some time at home to rest after a long quarter. I expressed my longing for the camaraderie of a sorority and how it would provide a sense of identity and belonging that I hadn't felt since matriculating.

It was only partly true. I didn't tell him I desperately needed to return to something familiar in order to recognize myself again because I couldn't appear to be overwhelmed or failing. Transferring wasn't an option, so I needed to appear to have everything under control. Overachieving was my identity, so I found a way to hide my unraveling behind that mask. He finally agreed.

From the bottom of the well, I was just looking for one brick to step on and another to hold onto. Then I'd stop and rest, knowing I was closer to reaching the top than I was before. Eventually, I'd look for another and another.

My time at home provided a few of those bricks. It became obvious to my parents that I was depressed in some way, but we didn't really speak of it. As the days passed, I found ways to push my thoughts deeper into the recesses of my mind and ignore the terrifying chatter. I focused on the familiar and found some equilibrium again through living with my parents and creating a daily routine.

As the fog lifted, I also became very aware of the fact that I was squandering a huge opportunity to study abroad or take on an internship, and I beat myself up for it on a daily basis. I perceived this self-imposed break as a sign of weakness that haunted me for years.

Despite these continued mental challenges, I was making my way out of that well. I returned to school in the spring, moved into a dorm on campus, and rushed a sorority. I also felt the bonds with my core group of friends growing stronger. I felt confident heading into my track season, motivated to make up for the time I'd lost all winter.

I looked for ways to branch out and find a new identity. I loved to sing and worship, and the gospel choir accepted me as one of only two white students among over 100 members. And while I may not have fit in on the surface, I felt more comfortable at choir practice than I did at my sorority because I could just be myself. There were no expectations. My inability to fit in felt freeing, while my inability to fit in at my sorority felt painful.

I also joined an all-women acting troupe called the Untamed Shrews. We traveled around campus, giving thought-provoking, feminist performances. I thrived off the panic attacks just before each show because I preferred feeling the intense but short-lived physical sensations instead of the constant mental chaos and confusion.

I had panic attacks in choir as well, but I was living my life in color again rather than shades of gray. As these parts of my life came into focus, it was like another brick I could stand on and pull myself up a little closer to the light. But when life seemed back on track, there still remained a constant sense that the anxiety or depression could creep back in at any moment. I didn't know what would trigger it—a thought, a memory, a dream. I realize now that my fear of anxiety was becoming as intense as the fears that caused the anxiety in the first place. I was now fighting a war on two fronts.

At the time, my objective knowledge about anxiety could be fit onto the head of a pin. It was purely a subjective experience for me. My disorders had already taken root, and I was in a particularly vulnerable period of my life. The environment, the cognitive dissonance, and the unhealed childhood trauma were all contributing to a confluence of factors that opened that box in the back of my mind, allowing those thoughts and fears to escape and multiply unchecked.

Chapter 8

Bricks and Mortar

"You can't always control what goes on outside.
But you can always control what goes on inside."
—Wayne Dyer

DURING MY JUNIOR year at Dartmouth, my best friend and I moved into our sorority house and were assigned the bedroom at the top of the stairs. Not down the hall or around the corner, but the first bedroom you reach if you find your way into the house. This made me very anxious. I tested the lock on the door daily and was very focused on the fire escape outside our only window, always plotting my escape.

One Wednesday after our weekly house meeting, as my sisters were leaving the house and returning to their rooms, I was summoned back downstairs.

"There is someone outside looking for you!"

I pushed my way through the crowded doorway, excited to see who had come all the way off campus to find me. The front walkway led to the road and cut through a hedge just before the sidewalk. As the crowd cleared, I saw him. He was leaning against his car at the break in the hedge, staring at me. I wasn't sure what was happening. I didn't recognize him, but in a split second, I replayed the last month in my mind. Expressionless, I slipped back into the house shaking but still breathing. It was the first time I saw his face, and I will never forget it.

I walked up the stairs to my bedroom without blinking. I opened the door, stepped inside, and closed it behind me.

"Who was it?" my roommate asked. "Wait. Are you OK?"

I walked to our only window and checked the lock.

"What are you doing? Are you OK?"

"He's outside," I replied, still staring out the window.

"What?"

"HE… IS… OUT… SIDE."

"Holy shit!" she said and locked our bedroom door.

The letters started on a Tuesday. I remember because my mother's letters always arrived on Tuesdays, so I looked forward to checking my box for mail as soon as I was done with lunch. But this time was different. This time I didn't recognize the handwriting. I opened the envelope to find a very personal letter from someone I didn't know.

He wrote about watching me at my track practices and following me to my classes. He described things he wanted to do to me and promised to contact me again soon. Then the emails started with more vivid details and anger at my lack of response. He recounted where I was at what time, what I was wearing, and who I had talked to that day. He said he was getting jealous of all the attention others were getting instead of him. He knew my work schedule, my class schedule, and my track practice schedule. He even knew what I had done during my workout that day, both inside and outside the practice facility, and promised to be there again tomorrow to watch me. It felt like he was literally under my skin, and there was no escape.

I lay in my bunk bed each night, remembering the warm feeling that window brought me when we first moved in. The fire escape comforted me, knowing I always had a way out. Now, that fire escape meant something very different. It had transformed from a way out to a way in—just like the windows changed after the robbery when I was a little girl. I lay there in the dark for hours with my eyes wide open, running through my day and wondering where he was hiding and why. What did he want from me? What was he capable of? How would this all end?

I dreaded the night as much as the day. As soon as I finally drifted off to sleep, he was standing there on the fire escape, staring at me through the window. Sometimes he would be in the room with the window open, my curtains blowing in the frigid breeze behind him. I would wake up with a jolt, lying in a pool of sweat, short of breath with my heart pounding. I lay there exhausted, not wanting to fall back asleep with no place to hide or feel safe.

After months of torment, little sleep, and constant anxiety, I felt myself drifting back into a fog. Before it was too late, I came to the realization that after fighting so hard to keep my head above water, I couldn't let someone push me back under. I was going to write the ending to this story.

I called my supervisor at work and told him everything. We met at the police station the next day. I filled out a complaint form and listened to my options. The detective told me I could just add my complaint to the thick file they already had on this man, or I could press charges, not knowing what the consequences may be.

I looked through the file and saw names I recognized. Some were my sorority sisters. And the stories they wrote were similar to mine.

One was the same girl who stood on those front steps and told me someone was out front waiting for me. It all made sense now. They were relieved he had moved on to someone else.

I asked for 24 hours to think it over, and the detective obliged. I lay awake the entire night wondering what he would do when he found out someone had finally pressed charges, and it was me. I stared at the window, wondering if he would find his way up. I wondered why his other victims had signed a form that they knew allowed this stalker to turn his deranged attention to someone else. Maybe it didn't affect them as much. I couldn't take that chance. What if the next girl took it worse than me? I couldn't live with myself. I had to make it stop.

The next morning, I walked to the police station alone, assuming he was watching me the entire time, with a sense of empowerment I hadn't felt in a very long time. I stood at the counter and agreed to press charges.

I signed the form, shaking with fear but with complete resolve that I was doing the right thing. I wondered if he would retaliate. I wondered if the girls in my sorority would think I was weak, given they hadn't pressed charges and were able to move on with their lives. I felt exposed and vulnerable, having no way of knowing the full consequences of the paper I just signed, so I walked straight to my track coach's office.

He was the largest, strongest man I had ever met, and I knew he would protect me. Until then, I had been ashamed to tell him. I thought he would tell me to wear different clothes and not attract attention. But now it had gone too far, so I told him everything. He was devastated and promised to keep me safe, not only at practice but everywhere on campus. And that is exactly what happened. Three weeks later, he called me into his office and told me that the man stalking me had been convicted and banned from campus ... forever.

One thing I learned during this ordeal was that I thrived in threatening, worst-case-scenario situations because I had been planning for them my entire life. So, for a short time, this felt like an opportunity to reclaim my power. But I didn't realize the collateral damage it was causing just under the surface. It triggered memories of the break-in when I was just 6 years old, as well as reminders of the existence of unknown threats beyond my control, feeding the beast in the shadows.

For months after, it was hard to stop thinking about him, even knowing he wasn't "allowed" on campus. I didn't entirely trust that the authorities on campus were keeping close tabs on him. But by the time I returned to campus my senior year, and I was living in a different place, I felt like it was finally over.

Just weeks into my senior fall, finally feeling safe in my surroundings again, I woke with such excruciating pain in my mouth that I called my father and begged him to come and get me. I told him I couldn't stand it and needed to come home. He left the house at 6 a.m. the next morning to retrieve me, and, with a lot of Motrin, we made it back home by lunch. It was a Friday, and we went to see my dentist that afternoon. My wisdom tooth was badly infected and needed to come out immediately. She scheduled my appointment for the following Monday and gave me pain relievers and antibiotics to reduce the pain and infection before surgery.

That night, I was excited to be home and had my boyfriend pick me up after weeks apart. On our drive, I reached down to change the radio station and heard a loud "pop." At first, I thought it was feedback from the radio, but then I felt a sudden and severe pain in the right side of my head. I looked down on my lap and saw broken glass glistening in the glow of the passing streetlights. I put my hand to my head—it felt sticky and wet. I thought I had been shot. My mouth was full of glass, and in my panicked state, I couldn't help but swallow. I started coughing and screamed, "There's glass in my mouth!"

"Oh my God! What happened? Don't swallow! Whatever you do, don't swallow it," he said.

I immediately swallowed again then started spitting as much as I could onto the car floor. By now, I was sobbing and disoriented. The car made a sharp U-turn toward the nearest emergency room. As the streetlights got brighter, I could see blood everywhere. When I opened the car door, the interior light revealed a large rock on the floor between my feet. Someone had thrown it through the passenger's window and struck me in the head.

After the nurses helped flush the glass out of my mouth and pick small shards out of my face, I sat on the examining table, waiting for CT scans to come back. Why would someone do this? Why would they stand on the side of the road and throw a rock at a car window, knowing I was on the other side of it? And then, all of those same feelings came rushing back in. Why would they take my tea set instead of my piggy bank? My fear of this unpredictable, uncontrollable, sometimes dangerous, and violent outside world that could infiltrate mine without warning was awakened again. I felt violated, vulnerable, and fragile. The cage door had been pushed open just enough to let the anxiety find its way back in, quietly and without permission.

The scans revealed a concussion and soft tissue damage that caused my jaw to freeze shut, and, as a result, the wisdom tooth surgery was delayed for weeks until it opened back up. It was symbolic of the paralysis this event triggered in me—feelings of chaos and calamity, fear of the unknown, and being exposed to dangers I could not protect myself against. The main theme of my senior year became my obsession with death. The fear of it was ever-present, and I became ever-vigilant against unrecognized bodily sensations and unknown risks that lurked beyond the walls of my dorm room. I started taking my pulse during classes, counting my breaths like sheep each night until I fell asleep, cutting my food into tiny pieces so I wouldn't choke, even quitting the track team to avoid traveling in a vehicle driven by a stranger or sleeping in places I couldn't be sure were safe.

This was the start of the real battle. I had already built my box, but I was now working overtime to reinforce its walls. I felt an urgency to protect myself against all unknowns, to limit myself to what I knew was safe, avoiding risk at all costs and anything that could trigger another panic attack or, worse, another plunge into that deep well of despair and depression. Things like adventure, excitement, happiness, joy, and fulfillment became secondary to predictability and security. As the war in my mind raged on, the walls grew taller and thicker.

The Difference Between You and Me*

I could strike a match
and burn this to the ground.

These dreams weren't that important.
I could just open my eyes and wake up.

I could blend in so easily you'd never see me again.
A new accent or dialect, and you'd never hear me again.
Just a change of clothes or scenery.
A shorter memory and longer hair.
Less insight and more inclination.

Just the flip of a switch and
I could rest in the darkness.
Just a warm steady breeze to shake this shiver.
Just a few degrees and my climate could change.

*All poetry woven throughout these pages are written by Wendy Tamis Robbins, unless
otherwise specified.

Just a slip in my grip and the sun would set
and these wounds would start to heal.
Just a little less strength
and my world would be gray—everyday.

Chapter 9

The Debate

"Too many of us are not living our dreams
because we are living our fears."
—Les Brown

"THE SEAT IS RIGHT DOWN FRONT, middle of the second row," she said. My heart fluttered, then sank. It had been the most exciting night of my life... until those words came out of her mouth and I knew I couldn't do it.

It was 1996 and six months before the election. I was working advance for Senator Kerry in his re-election campaign against the sitting governor, William H. Weld. I had gone from phone-bank volunteer to working with a team of paid campaign workers who prepared the senator for events like rallies, parades, and this, the first debate of the campaign at historic Faneuil Hall. I was a first-year law student, and I was ecstatic. I had dreamt of running for office since I was 12 years old, so this was my Mecca—the holy land. I had access to the candidate and inside workings of a campaign like I'd never imagined. The work was still more form over substance, but I didn't care. It got me close to everything.

That night, I had prepared the stage and watched the first half of the debate on TV monitors set up in the "war room." Once everything seemed to be running smoothly and there was nothing left for me to do, a senior worker pointed out that a campaign advisor sitting in the second row was leaving during the next commercial break. She asked if I'd like to take it. I stared down the center aisle of the main hall, located the seat, and started to sweat.

Just walk from here to there. That's all, I thought. I felt like Ichabod Crane staring at the bridge I needed to cross for safety. But in the back of my mind, I knew I was fooling myself. Walking through a full room of people was only the tip of the iceberg. I would never be able to sit in a seat in the middle of the second row. I was walking to my death. I didn't feel safe in the back row of a church, for God's sake, never mind the second row of a nationally televised political debate. But the clock was ticking, and I heard someone counting down. I started walking fast and excused myself past the first seven people seated in the row. I hit the seat hard with my heart pounding out of my chest. I made it. Now what?

"Three, two, one, and we're live!"

"Welcome back, Senator, Governor," said the moderator.

I looked at the calm smiles around me and wondered how I would ever escape. I had walked past seven on my left and counted six occupied chairs to my right. I was trapped. My heart raced faster than my mind, and the sweat in my palms was soaking the paper I was rolling over and over in my hands. I nervously asked the person next to me if I should exit to my left or right. He asked me to be quiet. The debate continued, and my discomfort became more apparent to those around me.

"Is something wrong?" asked the woman to my right.

"I think I need to leave," I whispered.

"What?" she looked at me strangely. "You can't get up while the cameras are rolling."

That put me over the edge. "You can't get up!" I repeated those words over and over in my head. It was like a cage door slamming shut with me the inside. I felt trapped, and I needed a way out. I couldn't make a scene in front of the candidates, my campaign co-workers, and everyone in the hall—but that's exactly what I did. Gasping for air, I shuffled past the six people sitting to my right with twelve minutes left in the debate. I walked straight to the back of the hall, out the doors, grabbed my coat and bag from the war room, and ran outside. I sat on the steps sobbing and screaming into the corners of Faneuil Hall square, "What. Is. Wrong. With. Me?!" I got up and paced, inhaling and exhaling, wondering how I was going to live my life like this. How would I ever realize my dreams? How could I show my face again at the campaign? Could I go back in and watch from the back of the hall without complete embarrassment?

I opened the door to the hall, and the crowd erupted into applause. It was over. I missed it and made a fool of myself again, and in front of people I idolized. If I couldn't sit in the second row, how could I ever be on that stage? My dreams were a joke. I wiped my face and never returned to the campaign again.

More afraid now than ever before of the dream-crushing paralysis my panic attacks could cause, they became more frequent. By my second year of law school, I was having them in class, on train rides to and from Boston, and in most social situations. I felt my fears resurfacing and needed to refocus on the walls I was building. They needed to be thicker, higher, and more perfect than ever to hide my symptoms and protect myself from triggers. I needed to take back control quickly if I was going to graduate. With no money to spare,

I took out a loan and moved into an apartment on Beacon Hill just a block away from school. Knowing the loan wasn't enough to cover my expenses, I took a job at the State House just a block in the other direction. And with that, my world felt safe and small again.

Chapter 10

The Replacements

*"To be nobody but yourself, in a world which is doing its best,
night and day, to make you everybody else—means to fight
the hardest battle which any human being can fight."*
—E.E. Cummings

BY MY THIRD YEAR OF LAW SCHOOL, anxiety was only affecting the perimeters of my life. I had retreated deep inside my box, systematically removing as many sources of anxiety as possible. But while I was mentally comfortable, I was at a tipping point physically. I found myself in unfamiliar territory, feeling imprisoned by my body rather than empowered by it.

I had started gaining weight the minute I walked through the doors at law school. There was more stress and less free time than I had imagined, so I ate what was convenient and comforting. Bagels, bagels, and more bagels were washed down with gallons of coffee—and cream and sugar. Anytime I felt anxious, I reached for food, caffeine, and alcohol, and gained over 40 pounds doing it.

My only workouts at the time were the walks from the train station up Beacon Hill with a thousand-pound pack full of law books strapped to my back. When I returned home from college, where I had trained for varsity track and field almost every day, I had stopped working out altogether. The rapid heartbeat and heavy breathing triggered panic attacks that I didn't want to have in a gym or on a run two miles from my house.

One day, I set out to find the tiny law school gym on the second floor of an apartment building on Beacon Hill. When I peeked in, there was only one person lifting weights and a lonely treadmill in the corner. I put my headphones on, set the treadmill to 20 minutes, and started to walk. By the third week, I started to jog. By the third month, I was running. Given I was the only person in the gym, and it was just across the street from my apartment, I wasn't afraid of panicking, so I didn't. I capitalized on this temporary reprieve. I found the Atkin's diet at the same time, and despite eating more cheese than I thought humanly possible, lost almost 30 pounds. I felt back in control of my body.

Unfortunately, this was at the same time I met Jack. Having seen the comments of those young boys in the fort reinforced over the years, I believed I could attract a man—*initially*. The challenge would be to face the disturbing belief it planted deep inside me that every new person presented an opportunity to be exposed and abandoned. They would fall in love and then find someone more physically attractive and turn the page. My efforts to take back control and convince my boyfriend otherwise mixed with my anxiety and perfectionism created a poisonous cocktail. Soon, my eating and workouts shifted from healthy to compulsive and destructive.

My first real evidence of men turning the page was the fear of it I saw at home. Even before I ever stepped foot in that fort, my mother's constant body-shaming and fear that my father was cheating on her were potent. I internalized the direct relationship between dieting and cheating. If your thighs are too big, he will cheat on you. Your appearance is unacceptable, and, therefore, you are unlovable and replaceable.

I started dating Jack while losing my last 10 pounds. The more he looked at other women, the more weight I lost. I was just following the formula—the bigger your thighs, the more likely he is to cheat or leave you altogether. Basic math. Unfortunately, he was a 28-year-old man who, for as long as I knew him, would never stop scanning his surrounding area for attractive women.

As the relationship continued, he actually complained about my body. He wanted me back at the weight I was when we met. It made no sense to me at the time. Was he purposefully sabotaging the relationship? He was turning my "basic math" into "fuzzy math." He lived with two other men, and I saw the Playboy magazines in their apartment. I knew that was their ideal. I was in the fort, remember? So, despite his objections, I was still convinced that I must not be thin enough yet, and math just wasn't his thing.

Just give it a few more pounds and he'll come around, I thought. *Then I'll be irresistible.*

I woke each morning thinking, *If I control myself and my weight today, I can control him and my relationship.* When he didn't act the way I wanted, which was most days, I went to bed with a pit in my stomach. *I'm still not good enough. Tomorrow I will restrict more and try harder.*

I thought more self-loathing and judgment would ignite more motivation and willpower to achieve my goal. I was trying to fit myself into the tiny shape I thought he *should* want, even though he was telling me otherwise. I was convinced he couldn't love me just as I was, and I was trying to convince him of it, too. And the more punishment I inflicted on myself to please him, the more damage I did to my own self-worth. I was destroying both my relationship with him *and* myself.

Ultimately, I was thin and still felt replaceable. The formula didn't work. The more I tried to present a perfect picture, the more he looked away. I didn't realize that my actions were breaking the connection, not my weight. Yet I internalized it as so: no matter what I looked like, there would always be someone more attractive, and I would never have the control I sought. I did all I could to achieve the perfect size, inflicting as much pain as possible trying to find it. Still, I was not loved. I was only lost.

This continued through all of my relationships and became a great source of anxiety. I had a panic attack every time I was with a man and saw an attractive woman. It was immediate, intense, and uncontrollable. I had convinced myself that upon seeing her, he would leave me. Just like that. It felt truly inevitable in the moment. I played it out in my mind so vividly that it triggered the same physical reaction that I would have had if it actually happened. When my panic attack ended, I claimed to know exactly what he was thinking and blamed him for my anxiety.

I made excuses for not wanting to go on vacations or meet up with friends. Even in church, I was hyper-vigilant—my fight-or-flight response triggered with adrenaline coursing through my veins and ready for battle. I would strategically position myself as a barrier or distraction once I identified the threat. I heard the bomb ticking as I waited for him to see her and my life to explode in front of me.

My mind was interpreting it as if it was actually happening. I thought this was normal for many years, not making the connection with other situations where an acute sense of "loss of control" caused me intense anxiety. I didn't realize that just as I was playing out the worst-case scenarios while driving through tunnels or over bridges, I was playing out those same scenarios in my relationships. Over time, those imaginary scenarios became my real memories. I thought, *Of course he will leave with her, because that's what always happens,* when in fact it had never happened at all.

This need to control my physical appearance continued for decades as my anxiety raged on. I thought this picture-perfect exterior would relieve my anxiety. When it didn't, I hope to at least hide it. But as my thighs shrank and my anxiety grew, the anxiety itself became the primary source of my self-loathing and what made me more replaceable than ever. The shame made me feel unworthy and undeserving of love on a very deep level. I was broken and unable to put my pieces back together, even with hard work and determination. I didn't recognize, much less *love* myself in this condition, so how could I expect anyone else to?

Chapter 11

The Rollercoaster

"One cannot think well, love well, sleep well,
if one has not dined well."
—Virginia Woolf

AS MY ANXIETY INTENSIFIED, so did my fear and shame. My loss of control over what was going on inside of my own body and mind created a manic need to control everything on the outside. I was desperate to hide my scary thoughts and mysterious physical ailments by making everything else look perfect. But the lines blurred over time, and my control became a form of self-flagellation. I hid behind the glaring light of perfection, and in its shadow, I regained my power by punishing myself. This is how my eating disorders fed off my anxiety.

Once I lost all the weight, I also lost any sense of a healthy relationship with food. I ate only carbohydrates—plain bagels, plain white rice, plain pasta, and lots of caffeine. If I made it through the day on only one bagel, I'd eat a candy bar before my ride home as a reward with the added benefit of having enough sugar in my system to get me through the drive.

Given my goal was to reduce and ultimately rid myself of anxiety, I couldn't have employed a worse strategy. Being on a caffeine-fueled deprivation diet would put *anyone's* body and mind on a rollercoaster. But for someone in my condition, it became a primary contributor to maintaining my anxious state.

Foods that are high in sugar (candy bars) and carbohydrates that are high on the glycemic index (bagels) increase your blood sugar levels. Likewise, stress can cause the body to produce hormones that make it difficult for insulin to do its job, which is to metabolize that sugar, so more stays in the bloodstream.[16] The highs and lows of my blood sugar and caffeine levels created more panic attacks than I can count.

I got on the rollercoaster at 7 a.m. when the stress of my drive from my parents' house into Boston sent a constant stream of adrenaline through my veins for at least an hour. Upon arrival, I rewarded myself for surviving with a large cup of coffee and a bagel. By noon, I was crashing—brain fog, eyelids closing, and stomach acid churning. Lunch was Diet Coke and another bagel or a salad. The rush of caffeine with such little food made my hands shake and my mind race until I came crashing down the other side again by mid-afternoon. I opened another Diet Coke to avoid snacking and got my final caffeine kick to make it through the end of the day. I'd panic the entire drive home, walk through the door hyperventilating and shaking, and drink a beer to calm down. And that was the best I would feel all day.

While the physical symptoms of caffeine and erratic blood sugar levels cannot be ignored, I also misdiagnosed my panic attacks for hypoglycemia for 25 years. I called it "bonking" and believed it was due to physical overexertion or lack of food. My heart raced, my hands and sometimes even my legs shook uncontrollably, an uncomfortable heat would wash over me and then radiate from between my ribs, causing sweat to break out. When I tried to inhale, it felt like someone was pressing a pillow over my face. My tongue seemed to swell as my throat closed, and the panic of not being able to eat or drink to alleviate my physical symptoms made me panic even more.

When I felt a "bonk" coming on, I tried to find sugar immediately. Juice, candy, alcohol, whatever was closest and appropriate at the time. I regularly had to pull over to convenience stores or gas stations and take a few sips of juice in the parking lot.

Before I realized these episodes were mental and not physical, I was always preparing for a bonk. I truly thought I could die if I didn't. This created a whole new source of anxiety that was directly caused by my diet. Anytime there was the slightest chance I may get stuck without food for an extended period—an elevator, plane, chairlift, boat, car, my sister's house, movie theater, kayak—I panicked.

This diet also exacerbated the stomach issues already caused by my anxiety. My doctor's office was only a block away from my office at the State House, and I was visiting two to three times a week. By mid-afternoon each day, my stomach had collected more acid than it could handle, and I was keeled over in pain. The doctor would hand me an entire bottle of Mylanta and tell me to drink it all.

I remember sitting in his office the week before I left for a trip overseas. I was tying myself in knots thinking about the plane flights. His advice to me was, "Go eat your way through Europe and calm down."

On another visit to my female gynecologist, I told her my eating and drinking habits, as well as my motivations, fears, and battles with anxiety. I told her I could hardly think straight most days the fog was so thick. Her advice to me was:

"Never compromise your mental faculties for weight loss. You've worked too hard and accomplished too much."

I will never forget that. I completely agree. But my issue was bigger than weight loss. My problem was my need to control what I looked like on the outside to hide the fact that I was unraveling on the inside. Not only was I trying to hide it from others, but now I was trying to hide it from myself.

Over time, eating anything gave me anxiety. I didn't know what or when to eat and feared my weight loss would vanish with the slightest amount of calories. Eating became symbolic of losing control. At the same time, not eating gave me anxiety because I feared bonking. I still thought the episodes were unpredictable and out of my control, which only perpetuated my fear of them. I was being torn apart at the seams.

The more chaotic my circumstances felt, the more toxic my relationship with food and my own body became. It was never more clear than when I started eating with a cup. Just thinking about binging and purging gave me anxiety, so that was never an option. And I beat myself up for not having the courage to do it, so I found another way. I chewed my food and then spat it out into a cup before swallowing. This makes absolutely no logical sense to me now, but at the time, it allowed me to relieve my desire to taste but deprived me of satiation. I actually researched whether you could gain weight by doing this. I was so blindly grasping for control that I had no perspective on how out of control everything had become.

When I was finally a size 2, I could no longer stand being in my own skin. I was constantly trying to distance myself from the battle that raged within. If I could have ripped my body off my soul like a pair of jeans, I would have. Existing in that constant state of pain grew more and more intolerable until finally, I was so exhausted that my resolve to maintain this masochistic control waned.

When you restrict your diet out of pain or punishment, you eventually exhaust yourself and eat. Sometimes you eat a lot, and it goes on for days or weeks. Then you gain weight and prove to yourself that it *was* all a lie, that you *don't* deserve to be a size 2, you *can't* be trusted around food, and you are completely out of control. And then, in an effort to regain control, you are back in the lose/gain cycle—back on the rollercoaster.

When I discussed my anxiety with doctors and therapists, my food and alcohol consumption were rarely discussed. The sugar, flour, processed foods, artificial sweeteners, alcohol, and caffeine were never identified as potential sources or even agitators of the various mental health issues with which I struggled. They were never considered as the direct cause of the bodily sensations that triggered the anxious thoughts that set the panic in motion.

That is, until one day, a doctor finally asked about my caffeine consumption. I was seeing him for my racing heart and palpitations. We had just completed days of tests, which had proven only that it was functioning perfectly fine. He suggested I stop drinking caffeine forever, knowing that caffeine caused similar symptoms that could be misconstrued and misdiagnosed by even the most discerning anxious minds.

At that point, a gust of wind would trigger a panic attack. We both knew that finding a magic bullet that could diminish my panic response was not realistic. But removing one factor that was likely causing two to three panic attacks a day was a good place to start. Desperate for relief, I removed caffeine from my life entirely, and it made an immediate and measurable difference.

But it was only the tip of the iceberg. The road to transforming my relationship with food and alcohol from dysfunctional to diagnostic, and eventually, to therapeutic, was one of the longest, most difficult, but also most important rollercoasters I've ever ridden.

Chapter 12

The Lifeline

*"Perhaps the greatest risk any of us will ever
take is to be seen as we really are."*
—Cinderella

THE SUMMER AFTER GRADUATION, it was time to take the bar exam. All
those years of dread—the tales of what one had to endure over those
two days of torture—and it was finally here. The long hours wore me
down quickly. Working full time and studying full time upset my
mental stability. My nerve endings felt like they were exposed, and I
cried nearly every night. As a result, my relationship with Jack grew
increasingly tumultuous.

Once the exam was over, the fear of not passing remained ever-present, and with the incessant studying behind me, I had plenty of extra
time to dwell on the potentially negative outcomes.

By August, I had run out of money to pay for my apartment, I had no new job prospects, I was stressed waiting for the exam result, my relationship was strained, and my anxiety was gaining momentum. So, I did what any logical Ivy League-educated lawyer would do. I moved back home with my parents.

My first night back would be humiliating, but it was also my mother's birthday, so at least I would have a distraction.

"Tomorrow's Mom's birthday," I said emotionlessly into the phone.

"Oh. Really?" My sister was never one to remember birthdays or anniversaries or any "special" day. Whereas I remembered them all and celebrated each one as if it were the first and the last all wrapped into one.

I invited her to the house for dinner, and she begrudgingly agreed. I knew she would much rather go about her day as if it wasn't happening and resented me for making it not only a "thing" but a thing for which I would get the credit—so turning the spotlight on me rather than Mom.

I could feel the anger building just below the surface on that call. But it wasn't until after the birthday dinner that I saw its full fury. I always had a need to talk to my family about what I experienced as a child. My hope was that they would confirm my memories were accurate and help me understand what had happened. No one seemed interested in reliving the past with me, my sister especially.

I also had a knack for bringing it up on otherwise "happy" occasions—birthdays, Christmas, Thanksgiving. Everyone was together, so it seemed logical. And I thought we would bond over the experience, not place blame and argue. I was wrong on all counts. I only had to hint at my mother's "episodes," and an argument ensued and escalated to a place I'd never been. There were years of anger and pain built up that exploded into rage. It was exhausting and unfortunate. It was a version of myself I had never experienced. I thought it was just the culmination of an extremely emotional and stressful summer.

When I woke for work the next morning, my eyes were swollen from crying, and my throat was sore from screaming. I grabbed my briefcase and started my commute into Boston. About halfway through, I felt pains shooting through my abdomen. I was sure it was the tension from the night before mixed with too much coffee on an empty stomach. The pain grew blinding to the point I pulled off the road. I could hardly breathe through the pain.

With my hands on the wheel, I closed my eyes and hung my head forward, inhaling through my nose. There was something terribly wrong—appendicitis, blocked colon. I reached for my phone to call my doctor but dropped it in a wave of pain. I watched it bounce on the floor out of reach. I started the car and drove straight to Massachusetts General Hospital. By the time I walked in the front door, I was delirious.

"Excuse me, Miss. Miss! Can I help you, Miss?!"

I walked right past my doctor's receptionist and into the first empty room I found.

"Can I help you?" the nurse asked.

"Something is terribly wrong. I can't breathe. The pain is unbearable." I cried and held onto my knees, pulling them to my chest.

She handed me a robe and stroked my back.

"Why don't you undress and fill this cup for me right there in the bathroom, and I'll be right back. I promise." She assured me everything would be OK, but I wasn't convinced.

I returned from the bathroom and curled up on the table, still holding my knees and crying through the pain.

"Good morning. I'm Dr. Meyers. I hear you are having some pain." She wasn't my doctor, but I didn't care. I nodded my head.

"Do you know you're pregnant?" she asked matter-of-factly.

"Excuse me?"

"You are pregnant."

The walls of the room warped around me, and a rush of heat enveloped my body. My future flashed before me, the bar exam results, the new job I hadn't found yet, Jack who was miles away on a work trip. A baby did not fit into any part of that equation.

She explained that more tests would be necessary, and they would take blood and rush me in for an ultrasound to determine if the pregnancy was ectopic. This would mean immediate surgery because the fertilized egg had attached itself somewhere in my fallopian tube, rather than in my uterine wall.

They sent me back into the waiting room, where I contemplated my options. Keep a baby with a man I didn't want to marry? Adoption? Abortion? I couldn't think straight. I was terrified. This decision would break me into pieces. I couldn't bear it. I knew that surgery was imminent if the ultrasound showed the pregnancy was ectopic, and I was all alone. I couldn't tell anyone this was happening. How could I be so careless?

With the tests complete, I was called back in to see the doctor. I was miscarrying. The decision had been made for me. I was off the hook. I felt overwhelming guilt for feeling grateful and a confusing and profound sadness. I was four months pregnant. I was pregnant when I took the bar exam. For weeks after, I cried for the baby I'd lost, but over time, the lines grew blurry. I didn't know who I was crying for anymore. I just kept crying.

What I did know was that I felt more alone than ever. I was too ashamed to tell anyone. How could I let this happen? How could I jeopardize everything I'd worked for? There were no boys stealing tea sets or throwing rocks to blame. This was all mine—my carelessness, my rage. My world was spinning out of control.

Rather than reach out for something stable, for someone to help, I isolated myself. I vowed never to bring up my childhood memories with my family again. They would be a burden I would bear alone.

I retreated from my boyfriend. Just looking at him reminded me of sitting in that waiting room, sobbing alone. I reinforced my walls to keep everyone in my life at a safe distance.

I took a few days off from work and thought about my next morning drive incessantly. I had taken the train during my first year of law school and was adamant about leaving unreliable and anxiety-inducing public transportation behind and driving myself. I made sure that my mobile phone was fully charged. At the time, mobile phones had only been around for about two years. I had inherited my father's first phone. It was a brick and would lose its charge frequently, despite being plugged into the car's cigarette lighter. The service was barely audible, and there was no such thing as a "hands-free" option. Unfortunately, those drives became terrifying, testing my ability to keep my job, and that phone became my lifeline.

The commute into Boston was mostly straight south on a highway that continued over the Tobin Bridge, a large double-decker truss bridge built in 1954 that spanned the Charles River and deposited its travelers at the foot of the Boston Garden. If I was lucky enough to make it to the bridge without incident, everything would surely fall apart there. I had created several "safe places" along the drive where I could pull off an exit into a parking lot, get out of the car, and find my breath again. But once I reached that bridge, there was no "safe place." There was always a wall of traffic and no breakdown lanes or exits. I never knew if I would sit there for 15 minutes or an hour. I couldn't stay calm under the pressure of having no way out and no way to be saved if something terrible happened.

The anxiety built as I approached the bridge, not knowing what I would find or how long I would be trapped. This created the explosive cocktail of stomach acid and adrenaline—another reason to get across that bridge as quickly as possible. The thought of not reaching a bathroom in time was certainly not calming. While this exacerbated the anxiety, my breath became so shallow that my hands tingled from the lack of oxygen and worked its way up my arms until they were numb. My "what if's" then spiraled out of control.

"What if I just stop and can't go any further, and the cars are backing up and the horns are honking, and people just pass me by as I faint and fall to the ground unresponsive?"

"What if I go to the bathroom in the car, in my work clothes, and can't get myself off this bridge and all the way back home?"

And there were thousands more. As my chest tightened, my mouth dried out, and my throat felt as if it was closing. I struggled to swallow and gagged as I gasped for air. I prayed out loud for help, some relief, just one deep breath, but struggled to verbalize as my tongue felt two sizes too big and thoughts of a stroke circled.

Then the yawning began as my body instinctively begged for more air but with no relief. But my stomach was so tight my breath only reached my chest, and my mouth would stay wide open with absolutely no air moving in or out. I was left empty and gasping for just short breaths.

When I finally made it over the bridge, I detoured directly to the State Police Headquarters just off the first exit. I stumbled in, day after day, and walked directly to the ladies' room in the lobby. It was the last safe place on my journey. I knew that if I needed help, the police would know what to do. This started my compulsion to always know where the closest hospital or acute care facility was located. I used the bathroom if necessary or just stood at the sink, grasping the porcelain with white knuckles. Eventually, I made it back to my car and arrived at my office exhausted. That was all before 9 a.m.

The thought of still having to manage the drive home would haunt me as I moved through my day, but I had one ace in my hand—I could call my mom. That wasn't an option in the morning when she was at work. But I knew that on most days, she would be free for me that evening.

Some days I called her the minute I reached the highway, hoping she'd stay on for the entire ride, while other days, I waited until the terrible thoughts started and panic set in. I would try to delay the call or pretend I was calling for something else because there was always a sense of embarrassment and shame that I was not in complete control of myself or my thoughts.

I prayed for light traffic or a distraction. Some nights, my mind ran so fast I couldn't get through a song on the radio. I kept changing the station, looking for some kind of relief. I was jumping out of my skin. I wanted to get out and run away from the car, from myself, and find peace. I wanted to be anywhere but where I was. There was so much energy behind the anxiety and fear. My fight-or-flight response was constantly triggered with no outlet, no release.

I would stumble to the front door with arms almost numb and legs so weak they could barely hold me up. But on most nights, I wouldn't have made it even that far without those calls with my mother. With compassion, she asked about what I was feeling and shared similar stories. She asked about my day to distract me. She walked me through some deep breaths and usually stayed on the call as long as I needed.

When I finally made it to the safety of my kitchen, the quickest way back to stability was beer. It quieted the voices in my head, stopped the shaking in my hands, and gave my legs strength again. Once I found that relief from what my brain interpreted to be a "near-death" experience, I felt euphoric having survived.

I didn't know at the time that I was training my brain to believe that my life was at risk every time I got behind the wheel of a car. Not because of any *real* threat, like a car accident, but because I believed the panic would kill me. If I had sat through the attacks and convinced myself I would live, they would have stopped. But instead, I gave them my power while I created crutches like "safe places" and "lifelines" that I needed to live through them. Which begs the question, what happens when they aren't there?

Chapter 13

The Medication

"Do what you can, with what you've got,
where you are."
—Theodore Roosevelt

MY RELATIONSHIP WITH ANXIETY medication was anything but romantic. I used Klonopin from start to finish. Nothing else was offered, and I never researched or asked for something different. First, because there were fewer options then, and second, because the thought of taking it or being dependent on it gave me even more anxiety. So, I used it only occasionally—situationally, I guess—on an "as needed" basis. Really out of pure desperation in an attempt to stop a runaway train. Its biggest effect on me was as a placebo. While the ingestion was sporadic, I couldn't leave the house without it. These little yellow pills were a crutch for 15 years.

The first time I was prescribed Klonopin was just after I graduated from law school. I was on a typical commute home from Boston with anxious thoughts about the traffic weighing on me. One of my favorite songs was playing on the radio. Normally I would be singing along, but not this time. My mouth stayed closed as the verses cycled through my head at a dizzying pace. My mind raced out in front of the lyrics—the song just couldn't keep up.

I turned up the volume in an effort to drown out the noise in my head, but it only got louder. It was as if I were turning up the volume on my anxiety. I changed the station again and again, but I couldn't settle on a song. I felt manic, frantically pushing buttons to find something that would calm me down. I wanted to jump out of my skin or out of the car, desperate to escape.

This wasn't my typical anxiety or a panic attack that had a beginning, middle, and end. It felt different, tireless, and building speed as if feeding off my fear. I had no idea what was happening or how to stop it. It was the moment my anxiety reached a frightening new level as I watched my mind spin out of control.

Twenty-four hours later, I was sitting in front of a psychiatrist, wondering if she could see my shattered pieces. She asked a series of questions about my anxiety that elicited one-word responses. I was too terrified to think about it, talk about it, or look directly at it for fear that it would escalate to the point where I could no longer bear to sit in her coffin-sized office.

She suggested meditation. It was then I realized I must have answered all of her questions wrong. I was clearly inept at communicating the immediacy of my pain to her. The sole reason for being in her office was that being with my own thoughts had become unbearable. To sit with them in meditation would be like walking into a burning house and sitting in the fire. But maybe she did realize how bad it was and knew meditation was exactly what I needed.

Regardless, I thought she should lose her license for even suggesting it. I feared it would overwhelm me, and I'd never find my way out.

I couldn't risk that, but I needed something to put out the flames before they destroyed me.

"Sorry. That is just not possible. I need help *now*," I responded as my hands began to shake and sweat. She reached for her pad, scribbled for a moment, and then handed me my first prescription for Klonopin 26 minutes into our session. We sat in silence. I looked at her, then the clock, then back at her again. I folded and refolded the piece of paper, turning and folding, turning and folding—the fear and shame of needing a prescription seeping into my fingertips and spreading throughout my body.

"I don't really need any more time, and I don't want to keep you. Should I just start taking the pills and come back next week?" I asked, looking back at the clock, turning and folding.

She squinted her eyes, paused, and then eventually nodded, "Sure. What works for you?"

By way of context, just over-the-counter drugs gave me anxiety, never mind prescribed medications. I psychosomatically manifested every possible side effect in the guise of a panic attack—throat closing, difficulty breathing, numbness, blurred vision, rash. But I felt like I was losing my mind, so side effects had become secondary, and my desperation now outweighed my reluctance. So, I jumped head-first into benzodiazepines.

Meditation, yoga, exercise, and sitting in one place were all impossible in that state of mind, so the medication felt like my only option. I used it regularly at first. The smallest dose calmed my nerves, slowed my thoughts, and relaxed my body—all things that had become impossible. I didn't feel drugged; I just finally felt normal again. It was a breath of fresh air. But just because taking that pill made me feel more comfortable in my own body doesn't mean I was ever comfortable taking it. I was desperate to stop the minute I started.

I took it periodically for years while I lived in my box, washing it down with a cocktail of water and shame. While I was never dependent on taking it, I was certainly dependent on taking it with me everywhere I went—*just in case.*

There was a Klonopin in every pocket I had—jackets, jeans, even pajamas. I ran them through the washing machine, collected them in the bottom of my purse, and clenched them nervously until they disintegrated in my sweaty palm. Just the thought of not having that lifeline with me triggered instant panic. So, they actually caused as much panic as they relieved.

Without Klonopin, I couldn't go to the hairdresser or dentist. Facials, manicures, pedicures, and massages were impossible. I couldn't sit through a church service, take transportation (trains, planes, cars, boats), go to a movie, a concert, a restaurant, or the gym. I couldn't be in social settings, whether with a group or one-on-one. I couldn't be alone with too much time on my hands. I couldn't walk through the woods or run around the block. I was dependent on something I wasn't even ingesting.

In the beginning, Klonopin served its purpose. It stopped the downward spiral. But it also made me feel more broken than ever—as if the moment she signed the prescription, it confirmed I was broken. While this drug was exactly what I needed to feel comfortable again in my own skin, I knew it wasn't a long-term solution.

Nonetheless, medication had its place in my recovery journey. It calmed me enough to see the walls I had built and realize that a dependency on it would have kept me on the inside looking out. The pills in my pocket could never be the answer. I would have to find freedom from anxiety with the weapons I'd find within, whatever that meant. I needed to find a way to face my fear of the anxiety and panic on my own. I needed to find the eternal source of peace and power that was hidden somewhere deep inside me.

During this time, the phrase "You are enough" caught fire. It was on the cover of magazines, on T-shirts, and on the lips of every self-help teacher, even Oprah. What I realized was that because of my anxiety, saying "I am enough" also had to mean "I am all I will ever need." In my battle, I don't need more armor, whether it was medication or any other lifeline. Once I found an inner peace and developed the ability to tap into it anytime and anyplace, I would have the power to find my way out of my box.

As I began to navigate my way out, one of my first goals was to leave my house without a pill—a full day at work, a walk around the block, or a trip to the grocery store. It took years to thoroughly distance myself from those little yellow tablets. But eventually, they were relegated to the back of my bathroom cabinet, where they sat for years, well beyond their expiration date, as a reminder of how far I had come.

Chapter 14

The Graduate

"Anxiety is the dizziness of freedom."
—Soren Kierkegaard

I FOLDED THE MORNING paper into a neat rectangle, opened the top flap of my black briefcase, and placed it inside. Staring into my bag, everything else disappeared for a moment. I realized the only thing that had changed since I became a lawyer was my bag and its contents. I'd gone from carrying a backpack bursting under the weight of my law books to carrying a leather briefcase holding the morning paper, a few fresh pens, and an updated copy of my resumé. Otherwise, I was the same person, same job, same walk up Beacon Hill to work, albeit now it was from the parking garage rather than my own apartment. My once-purposeful stride had recently become an aimless stroll. While the bag was lighter, the pressure to find a job and a purpose for all I'd accomplished was becoming more than I could carry.

It was clear now that I hadn't focused enough on what I would do after I graduated. I had no interest in joining a law firm. It was the equivalent of selling my soul to the devil at the time. I had to work in politics; I just didn't know how or where yet. Law firm jobs had a "track" for law students—a clear path to securing an offer. Jobs in politics and on campaigns were less "official" and predictable and more "know the right people and be in the right place at the right time."

I stopped and stared up the street toward the State House. *What has even changed since…* My thought was suddenly cut short by a siren screaming by and horns honking. The silence was broken, and the moment was gone. It was a depressing thought anyway, not a good way to start a Monday. I continued walking, stumbling at times.

These damn cobblestones! Paul Revere obviously never wore heels. Actually, I think he did. The thought brought an unexpected and refreshing smile to my face.

It was another summer day on Beacon Hill when everything slowed to a painful halt. The only redeeming quality that the State House in the summer afforded was the tremendous influx of interns. The hallowed halls were full of new, wide-eyed college students who saw government with fresh eyes and naive ideals. My colleagues and I used to see it that way, and the interns reminded us of what had once brought us there.

It was the idea that you could make a difference. At least that's what it was for me. Politics was going to be my opportunity to inspire people. To live my dream of making a positive change and showing others what is possible. I would gladly carry that torch. It was the resounding voice that whispered in my ear and drove me to be a part of something bigger than myself. This is where I would find it—under that majestic dome on the hill. At least that's what I once thought.

Since passing the bar exam, I had sent more resumés to and been on more interviews with elected officials, government agencies, and lobbying firms than I could remember. Some of the positions offered dream jobs, while others would require me to sell out completely. Another day with no calls, no leads, and no new ideas was becoming too frequent and, frankly, unbearable.

No one who knew me or even knew *of* me would have ever expected that I would still be without a great job, least of all, me. It had gotten to the point where every friendly face brought the unanswerable question, "What's going on with you? I thought you would be in D.C. by now. Are you still at the State House?" It had become so painful to try and answer these questions that I avoided friends, acquaintances, and even family. Isolation was the only way to protect against the pain and shame that came from confrontation.

While I knew that this posture wouldn't win me a popularity contest, I didn't realize how deeply affected I would be by the lack of connection to… anyone. I couldn't take a job I didn't believe in because of outside expectations, but bearing the pressure alone became, well, agonizing.

In the dark, quiet, and scary moments, Grace reminded me that, "This is not a race. When I am 40, successful, and happy, I won't remember how long it took to get this first job. I will only remember that I made it through an extremely difficult time in my life, and I'm stronger for it. I never did this to compete with others. It was always about what *I* wanted, whether those ideas conformed with those of my peers or not, should be of no consequence."

I tried to internalize that to justify and make sense of my nontraditional track through law school and current uncomfortable position. There was no logical next step if I wanted to move on from the State House. Searching for a new path would be uncharted territory.

I thought that if I didn't know how to get from A to B, or wondered what B even was, I should ask someone who was much further through the alphabet than me. Between law school and the State

House, I had collected several incredibly accomplished and well-connected mentors. These men had long, successful careers in politics both on the national and state level. We met over lunch or coffee, and most of the time, I left with either more questions than answers or an invitation for something completely unrelated to my career. The list of mentors was impressive, but my results were not.

At one such meeting, I straightforwardly asked, "So, from your perspective, based on my education and experience thus far, what is my next logical step?"

"Have you ever been to Croatia?" was the response my question elicited.

My first thought was that there must be government internships, or maybe someone was going over to teach a class on democracy.

"No. Why?" I responded with excitement in my voice. He lit up.

"Well, I'm thinking of going for a few weeks. Maybe even a month, just to get away and decompress before the next session starts. My wife doesn't like to travel that far anymore, so I wondered if you'd like to come with me."

My immediate reaction was complete shock. I didn't blink, and my mouth was stuck agape. The most powerful people I knew were men, so that's who I reached out to. I went to them for counsel and was met with inappropriate, unsolicited advances that had nothing to do with my career. Or maybe they had everything to do with it. Maybe I had fooled myself into thinking someone may actually offer a job or recommendation, or just a lead for an interview. I thought this was how it was done.

After the shock wore off, I felt ashamed to be there, as if I had done something wrong and brought it on myself. Was I sending mixed messages? I thought that because these men were married and between 10 to 35 years my senior, it was obvious these were professional meetings. I had brought my resumé, for God's sake. Had they reduced our relationship to the hope of a sexual encounter, or was I simply unemployable? Neither was a reality I wanted to digest. I felt completely betrayed by the very men I revered.

The clock was ticking, and I had absolutely nothing to show for my Ivy League diploma and law degree. I had the same job, and now, unable to pay rent, I had the same room I grew up in back in my parents' house. To top it off, I had stories of these disappointing networking efforts and fruitless interviews.

But I also had someone who always loved to listen to those stories. I only saw him periodically, but Tony was always eager to catch up on what he called "my wild ride." I found I could completely open up with him. Unlike all of the other people in my life, I felt no pressure to perform, no judgmental stares, no patronizing tilts of the head, no absurd comments about becoming a make-up artist instead of a lawyer. I had no fear and no filter with him—until now.

"Your face is like a breath of fresh air," he said.

"Oh," I blushed, accepted him into my embrace, and took a deep breath. I had lost that sense of myself over the last year—that pretty, happy sense. I had thought only of survival—of what I would do and where I would go—never of being still and light and hopeful, and even loved. I was only frantic and empty and caving in on myself with fear and despair. Hugs were typically dangerous territory for me, evoking too much emotion from my past, but I was so numb I didn't react at all. I closed my eyes and stayed in his arms for just a few extra seconds, and he felt it. He backed up and took a good long look into my eyes. It was a sure way to see into my soul, especially with tears welling up in them. He sensed a rawness to my pain and knew to proceed cautiously.

"So, where do you want to go? Are you hungry, thirsty?" he asked.

"I'm a little cold, so why don't we go grab something warm to drink?"

"Fine." He wrapped his arm around my shoulder and pulled me close as we started to walk. I could feel the tears overflowing now as the first one ran down my cheek, breaking the seal. Tony looked straight ahead as if to give me time and space to compose myself and settle into feeling close to someone again, even if it meant also feeling exposed. He led me to a cozy coffee house on the corner of Boston Common and started talking, sensing that if he didn't, I would be content to just sit in silence.

"So, where to begin? I mean, I'm always the same. Accountants don't change much. Audit here, tax return there, e-mailing auditor jokes to everyone I know... same bullshit. So, you go. You're always changing and creating great storylines for me."

I searched my recent past for a place to start, but everywhere my mind landed made my eyes well up again. The countless trips to Washington, D.C., no one called... my trip to New York City, didn't get the job, the trip to Europe with Jack. God! To think that talking about my miserable love life would actually be the *least* painful topic. I shuffled through pieces of a big puzzle that created a picture I didn't recognize.

"Well," I paused. It seemed like forever, as if I'd forgotten it was my turn to speak. "I guess I should just give you the highlights and go from there." I took a deep breath through my nose and felt the intense burn the tears had left. "Actually, do you mind if I run to the bathroom? Thanks."

My feelings were overwhelming me. This was a bad idea. If I couldn't even be with Tony, I was completely alone. I panicked at the thought. My mind was going blank just trying to find something to say to him when I returned. I felt trapped and paralyzed, knowing the anxiety would soon be too much to handle in such a public place. My breath became forced as I walked to the bathroom awkwardly, my motor functions starting to slow due to the lack of oxygen.

"Just let me make it to the bathroom," I pleaded with myself. I fell into the door with desperation and banged my way into a stall. I shut the door, barely able to secure the lock. I crashed down to the toilet seat, putting my head in my hands and taking deep breaths until the worst of the panic passed.

I left the stall and stood in front of the mirror, clinging onto the sides of the porcelain sink. "If you can't pull yourself together here, there is no hope. You will be stuck in this job living at home with your parents forever. Either tell him everything you are feeling or PULL IT TOGETHER." I chose the latter. I put up my walls, dried my eyes, walked slowly out of the bathroom, and returned to Tony.

"You OK?" he asked.

"Yeah, of course," I replied. I took a deep breath, looked him straight in the eyes, and forced a big smile. It was my only hope of reconnecting and regaining some sense of balance.

"I've got lots of options. You know me. Lots of connections, so lots of options. It's my first *real* job, so I need to be a little selective." I kept it positive and general to avoid any follow-up questioning.

"Well, that's great! Sounds like things are moving in the right direction," he replied.

"Absolutely."

The burning in my throat and nostrils intensified the bigger I smiled. The tears were back, and I struggled to keep my voice from cracking under the emotions that were erupting just below the surface. Now I was lying to my closest friend. I was hiding my failure to avoid the embarrassment and shame. I lied about a bright future rather than expose the black hole I was staring into. I smiled to reinforce that I was on the right path while convinced my life had become a dead end.

Before I lost control, I managed to pivot the conversation back to him with, "What about you? Tell me what's up with you?" I felt completely alone and isolated sitting right next to him. I desperately wanted him to reach out and wrap me in his arms where I could fall to pieces, knowing he would put me back together. I silently pleaded for him to ask more questions and dig deeper below the surface.

But others rarely do, whether they see the pain or not.

Chapter 15

Lost at Sea

"Don't look for the blood-soaked knees.
Find the wounds that no one sees."
—Men

WHEN I FINALLY received my first job offer, it was for a position that I never applied for. A letter arrived in the mail inviting me to interview for a clerkship with the Connecticut District Court. I was confident there had been a mistake because a clerkship is typically a stepping-stone to joining a law firm, and if I could barely make it through my day in familiar surroundings with family and friends, how could I possibly move to Connecticut?

Nevertheless, I was desperate to move on from the State House and out of my parents' house, so I took it. I moved 100 miles away into a 500-square-foot apartment in the middle of nowhere. I didn't know a single person in the entire state. My parents helped me pack, gave me a hug, and set me adrift.

Sitting on my couch surrounded by boxes, I was full of mixed emotions—my mind racing and heart pounding. What had I done? I felt trapped, like I wanted to run into the parking lot waving my arms for them to come back and take me home, but I knew I couldn't.

At least the apartment looked just as it had on the Internet—clean and sterile. It reminded me of my institutional dorm from sophomore year at Dartmouth and was already making me feel the same way—detached and isolated. A silver lining came just a week after I moved in, when my boyfriend was accepted to Columbia Business School. He would be in New York City come January. With my parents still near Boston, I could swim back to either shore if necessary.

But it was only September, so, until January, I was all alone. The first few months were a blur. My intrusive thoughts made the trip and followed me everywhere. The lack of distraction and unbearable stretches of silence were fertile soil for them to plant seeds of catastrophe. They taunted me with things I could fall victim to alone, including myself. My mind was either struggling to push these thoughts back into the shadows or overwhelmed and completely blank. At times, I felt like I was living in a dream or a movie. Some days I could hardly recognize myself in the mirror. And when I tried to exercise to get back into my body and feel something, just a walk outside or a minute in the gym, I'd have a panic attack.

I dreaded weekends because I didn't talk to anyone in person except the cashier at the grocery store. I'd call my boyfriend and parents and then count the minutes until Monday morning. It's said that idle time is the Devil's playground, and this was especially true for my anxious mind.

The Christmas holiday provided much-needed relief. The drive was unbearable, of course. I hyperventilated for hours, pulled off the road to catch my breath, stopped at gas stations for sugar and a toilet, and called my mother more than once. It took me twice as long to get there than it should have, but when I arrived, it was like the first breath of air I'd taken in months. The dissociation dissipated, and I was able to put on a happy face and pretend nothing was wrong. And my mother never mentioned the calls.

I returned to Connecticut, looking forward to knowing that I now had a second shore of safety to swim to that was just a train ride away at Columbia. Unfortunately, it was a rocky one. The relationship had been strained for many months. His own anxiety and need for constant reassurance created a dynamic where I didn't feel comfortable talking about the anxiety that resurfaced after the miscarriage and how bad it had become over the last year. I focused my attention on helping him get into business school as a distraction. As a result, our relationship was still based on a former version of me where I took care of him emotionally, and it was becoming more than I could bear. My biggest motivation now was not to save *us*, but to save myself.

The first time I visited him in the city was Valentine's Day. I hoped that being settled into business school would give him the confidence he needed to let go just enough so I felt safe revealing my own mental state. While I had imagined a romantic dinner on the Upper East Side where I could open up and we could reconnect; instead, I found myself in a pizzeria with his study group friends. I sat with these strangers pretending I was listening to their stories, all the while thinking about the end of my relationship and what that meant for me. When it all became too much, I stood up and asked to go back to his dorm. He agreed, but instead of going back to his room where we could talk and I could calm down, he took me to the lobby where the Young Republicans were having a party. I went directly to the box of wine on the folding table and filled my plastic cup to the rim. By 10 p.m., we were squeezed into his twin bed, no conversation, no connection, no hope. I lay awake all night, my head propped against his desk because he stole the only pillow, and plotted my escape from New York—and the relationship.

I arrived back in Connecticut late Sunday night, having just broken up with him, feeling untethered and lost. The next morning, I awoke to an envelope that someone had slid under my apartment door. Was he here to beg me to come back? Had he slept in the hallway all night? I was excited by the thought of a new beginning and opened the door. I looked down the hall in both directions and saw only morning newspapers scattered along the floor. I closed the door and opened the envelope.

My rent was increasing. My heart sank. I did the quick math and realized I couldn't afford it. The property manager had delivered an obligatory notice effective immediately… and effectively evicting me. The letter in my hands started to appear translucent, and the room began to spin. My debt was piling up faster than I could manage, my student loans were still in deferral, and my car payment was soaking up far too much of my modest paycheck. I had nowhere to go. I dropped the letter on the floor and noticed how loudly the clock in my kitchen ticked.

There was nothing left to do but pray. I dropped to my knees on the soft carpet and prayed. Then I prayed the entire ride to work. Overwhelmed by the thought of having no place to go and no way to find one, my mind went blank. That sent my heart racing because the only thought I had was that I'd get lost on my short drive to the courthouse. I pulled over four times to regroup, breathing deeply and looking around for reminders of which street came next.

I stayed at my desk through lunch, too anxious to socialize. But when I overheard one of my fellow law clerks mention her mysterious boyfriend from England was finally moving to Connecticut, my ears perked up. They had found an incredible (and affordable) apartment on the first floor of an old Victorian house. It sounded amazing. It was exactly what I needed and would never be able to find on my own. I missed the rest of her story, absorbed in my own housing panic.

Two days later, she walked into our windowless office in the middle of the courthouse and declared she'd broken up with him and backed out of the lease. I asked for the landlord's information and signed the lease just three days later. It felt like a miracle—like the big, deep breath I needed. My parents agreed to help with my move. They would rent a U-Haul and drive it all the way down to Connecticut. I was surprised at this grand gesture and how quickly it rolled off their tongue, but it all made sense when they arrived at my apartment the following month.

Why would they rent such an enormous truck? I thought. Didn't they know I would be living in just 500 square feet? When my father opened the back, most of their belongings were inside, with some space left over for mine. I was confused. Were they moving in with me?

"We are moving to Florida!" my mother said with excitement in her voice and a hint of trepidation. I didn't take my eyes off the boxes. I was stunned.

"What?! What about the house? Where will you live?" I asked, still staring at the boxes.

"Well, we've been planning this for a while, and we didn't want to add to your troubles, and your sister and brother seemed fine with it. You'd love the family that bought it. You really would. We bought a great house in Venice. We wanted to leave last year, but we waited for you to get settled, and with your new place, it seemed like the perfect time."

I finally looked back at them. "What?" Their faces didn't even look familiar anymore. I was completely numb. I couldn't let her words in. I drew the blinds and kept them on the outside of my walls for as long as possible. It was too much to comprehend. I needed to just keep moving and save the unraveling for later.

As I watched the U-Haul pull away, I hoped that my new surroundings would help take my mind off the loss of my boyfriend and my parents—my safe places. I would focus on creating my own safe place, not a sterile apartment, but something that felt like my own. I thought it might calm my nerves, help lift the fog, and give me a sense of self again. While there were moments of relief, they were fleeting at best. I tried to hold onto them with everything I had, but when the bright moments dimmed, the sadness overwhelmed me. This wasn't going to be the savior I'd been praying for.

I fell into a deep well of despair where the dread of nothing specific washed over me every morning and stayed until I fell asleep each night. I'd experienced vertigo before, but now it lasted weeks at a time. It made me weak and sick to my stomach. My fear of feeling this way forever seeped into my bones until they ached. My anxious and intrusive thoughts erased my past and future, so I was left looking at my life through a tiny lens that could only focus on the task right in front of me. I'd complete each one with no intention or identity, no sense of who I was anymore or why I was doing it. I moved from moment to moment, alone and scared and just surviving. Then some thought would trigger me, and in an instant, my breath was stolen. No air in or out, my heart raced faster than my mind, my limbs tingled, my heart dropped into my stomach, and alone and helpless, I feared the worst—death.

There was nothing left to do but pray. I dropped to my knees on the hardwood floor and prayed. "God, please, I beg you. Please calm my mind and stop the spinning. I want to let go and find peace in you. I don't know how to control it. I'm begging you to make it stop. Please."

I prayed all day until the prayers trailed off into tears, and finally, sleep.

The Red Floor

If drops of blood
stained every spot on the floor
where I fell to my knees and prayed,
with my eyes closed tight,
my hands holding my head,
every inch of that floor would be red.
When tears wash it clean,
I appear unaffected,
but my scars are a painful reminder
of knees still left unprotected.

Chapter 16

The Recount

"To venture causes anxiety, but not to venture is to lose one's self..."
—Søren Kierkegaard

IN NOVEMBER OF 2000, the presidential election was hanging in the balance, waiting for the Florida recount. I was still barely hanging on in Connecticut. I had overstayed my one-year clerkship because, once again, I had no other options. The only opportunity that had presented itself was at a law firm in Hartford, which is exactly where I said I'd never go. But I wasn't just drowning in anxiety anymore. I was drowning in debt, which made the idea of a law firm paycheck almost digestible.

Then I received a phone call. It was Michael Dukakis, the 1988 Democratic presidential nominee. He was asking me to go to Florida to help with the recount. I had met Michael when he and his wife, Kitty, attended events at the Greek foundation my great uncle had founded in Boston. We had talked about my political aspirations over the years, so he thought I'd jump at the chance to be part of such a historic event.

The room started to spin as I listened to him paint the picture of what was happening down there. I knew it was an amazing opportunity to be on the ground working shoulder to shoulder with my politic peers. I asked about transportation and housing, and he said I'd have to find my own way down, and that everyone was just sharing the cost of cheap hotel rooms.

I exhaled and felt the pressure in my chest release. I had just heard my excuse. My student loans were still in forbearance, and I couldn't make my rent or car payment without charging everything else in my life on credit cards. How could I possibly afford to pay my way to Florida and stay for an unknown period of time with people I didn't know in a cheap hotel? Not to mention asking for that time off from my clerkship, which would have required me to quit.

I called my father and he agreed, sort of. He told me I needed to do what was in my heart. So I checked my heart and it screamed, "Quit this awful clerkship and get to Florida! Charge it all to MasterCard. Stop thinking and go!" That voice was immediately drowned out by my anxiety, whose voice grew louder and clearer. "This is a ridiculous idea, and it's never going to happen. You are mentally, physically, and financially fragile. You are unbalanced and broken. You would never do something so risky and with such uncertainty." But the thought of going without knowing what could happen actually excited me. I felt like my future could be forever changed—exactly what I had been waiting for.

As I contemplated my decision, feeling the push and pull of my heart and my anxiety, I remembered a similar call I got in October of 1996. It was 11 p.m. when a law school friend asked if I could take a few days off from school to accept a paid position on Al Gore's campaign doing advance work at the vice-presidential debate in St. Petersburg, Florida. I was terrified of flying but needed to make up for what I'd done at the last debate. I needed to prove to myself that I could overcome my anxiety and live my life based on my dreams, not my diagnosis. I accepted immediately and my plane tickets and credentials arrived just a few days after. Unfortunately, a hurricane was headed into the Gulf of Mexico the day I was scheduled to leave.

I boarded the plane and walked all the way to the very last row. My ticket was booked just two days prior, so it was the only seat available. The hurricane had been downgraded to Tropical Storm Josephine that morning, but as we approached Florida, I wasn't taking any chances and sat in the back galley with the flight attendants who had been ordered to remain buckled in their seats for the remainder of the flight. I cried while they did their best to console me. My only redeeming thought was that I would die taking a chance to actually live my life rather than dying of a panic attack in my bedroom after having turned down the invitation.

When we finally touched down, I was exuberant having survived the flight. At baggage claim, I found a man holding a board with my name on it and suddenly felt very important. As we drove over the causeway toward St. Petersburg, waves crashed over the car, flooding the road beneath us. About halfway over, we turned back to find an alternative route. I didn't know what was worse, feeling helpless on the plane with the wind tossing us around like a toy or feeling helpless in the back of a car that was being overcome by an angry ocean.

Arriving in my hotel, I went to bed immediately, completely exhausted and vowing never to get on a plane again.

The next day was the debate, and there was a lot of work to do. I was in meetings with people I'd admired for years, Donna Brazil and George Stephanopoulos, but I said nothing. I was not invited to say anything, just to make sure microphones were working, flags were hung, water glasses on the podiums were full, and the Secret Service had everything they needed. Administrative, maybe, but it was a dream come true. I felt in control, following my heart despite the storms raging inside and outside of me.

Now, standing in my apartment with the phone still in my hand, that felt like a distant memory. I remembered that girl who dared to step out from behind the walls and live in the light for a moment. She wanted me to do it again now. She begged me to. But those walls were too tall and thick. The deeper I retreated into my box, the further she faded away. A wave of intense shame washed over me as I watched this once-in-a-lifetime opportunity slip away, taking my dreams with it.

"Well, let me know if you change your mind," Michael said. "I hope you find your way down there because they need all the hands they can get." *Michael Dukakis thought I was needed.* It was as if my entire life led to that phone call and I was paralyzed.

I hung up the phone and cried as the walls of my apartment closed in around me.

Chapter 17

The Storm

"When you learn to survive without anyone,
you can survive anything."
—Anonymous

WHEN I WAS COMMUTING around Connecticut, I called my mother every day. But for longer drives, staying on the phone for hours wasn't an option. I needed different tactics to get through those long stretches—those places in between when it was just as far to turn back as it was to keep going.

I packed food and identified "safe places" to stop and take enough deep breaths to buy me another 20 miles or so. I also started listening to inspirational and spiritual CDs that my mother would send to distract and calm me.

It was my second Easter in Connecticut, and I was meeting family in Newport, RI, for the weekend. I packed the car with a chicken breast and chocolate for bonking, plenty of Diet Coke, and CDs. I stopped several times along the way, prayed a lot, and never called my mother. I picked up the phone several times but worked through the panic and managed to make it on my own. I arrived around 7 p.m. on Friday and walked into the first restaurant I came upon, feeling completely spent. I wasn't meeting anyone until the next morning, so I had all night to acclimate and decompress. I sat at the bar, ordered a beer, and thanked God that the Red Sox were playing on the big screen TV to distract me.

By the time I ordered my second beer, I had met Greg, my first husband. He walked in with his roommate and some friends, and before I knew it, I was an honorary member of their group for the night. It provided a much-welcomed distraction from my last three hours alone on the road.

He lived in Newport, so this began several months of traveling the Route 95 corridor between Hartford and Newport. I was always surprised at the lack of lights, exits, and phone reception during those long stretches. I didn't want to speed, but I felt like I was forced to run from one end to the next just to find civilization. I employed the same tactics I did for those drives back home and added Diet Coke and Raisinets to the mix. While I thought these would keep me awake and focused, in retrospect, the caffeine and sugar could not have been a worse cocktail for my anxiety.

The excitement to see this person I had fallen completely in love with pushed me through countless panic attacks—on and off the road—and by August, we were engaged.

One Sunday in September, feeling the summer slipping away, I stayed in Newport a little later than usual. The sunset was beautiful as I drove over the Newport bridge. I considered my three-hour drive in the dark with some trepidation, but having not looked at the weather before I chose to extend my stay a few hours, I was oblivious to what Mother Nature had in store.

My rain phobia had not been resolved by the time I crossed over that bridge into the abyss that was the stretch of highway between Newport and New Haven. As I crossed the border into Connecticut, it was already uncharacteristically dark for that time of day. For most of the way, the only source of illumination came from my headlights. Just when I thought it couldn't get any darker, the world seemed to lose all light. What I didn't know at the time was that I was driving directly into the path of a ferocious storm.

The rain was light at first and then intensified as the winds grew stronger. My breath grew shallow as I feverishly turned the radio dial, searching for a weather update. I found nothing that warned of the severe thunderstorms and tornados moving into the area that I called the "dead zone." It was the stretch of I-95 where radio stations went to static and cell service vanished.

Finding no help from the radio, I picked up my phone to call my mother. It had 20 percent battery left and only one bar of service. I scrambled to plug it into the cigarette lighter to charge, and nothing happened. No red light. My heart sank. I wiggled it around, pulled it out, and slammed it back in, desperate to make a connection, but nothing happened. I held off using it as long as possible, but in a short time, the panic was racing through my veins. Water flooded my windshield faster than my wipers could handle. My headlights struggled to penetrate the torrential sheets of rain. With no billboards, gas stations, guardrails, or even a bright divider line on this two-lane stretch of highway, I struggled in the darkness. I could only tell I was on the right side of the road when an oncoming car passed, and the headlights made me swerve back into my own lane.

I tried dialing the phone with one hand but hit all the wrong buttons and dropped the phone. After 10 minutes of frantic fumbling, I finally completed a number. After just two rings, the call failed. I had 8 percent battery left and dropped the phone into the passenger's seat.

Devastated, I felt my chest tighten and my throat close. I struggled to inhale. Then the rain (and subsequent noise it brought) subsided for a moment, and I heard a faint voice say, "Hello?"

It was like putting an oxygen mask over my mouth. I put the phone on speaker and yelled, "Mom?! Can you hear me? Mom!"

"Just barely. What's all that noise?"

"It's crazy here right now. I'm driving back home, and I hit this storm and I can't see anything, and I don't know how bad it is up ahead and there is no place to pull over and I'm having a lot of trouble breathing and I still have over an hour to go and I'm not sure I can make it," my thoughts were pouring out of my mouth stream-of-consciousness. In just that short time, the rains turned torrential again, engulfing my car. "Can you check the weather and tell me how long it's going to last?" I raised my voice louder and louder as the rain fell with brutal force as if it intended to shatter my windshield. "And hurry, I don't have much time. Service is spotty, and my batt—Mom? Mom?!"

Silence. I looked down at the phone, and it was dead. The service hadn't failed; it was the battery. All hope of a connection with the outside world was gone. I was completely alone in this storm, with no information and no escape. No lifeline in the face of a panic attack, or a heart attack, or a car accident. It was too much to process, and I spiraled out of control. My breathing deteriorated. I felt like I was trapped in a coffin that was sinking into the ocean. I was convinced I would surely die before this was over.

About 15 miles down the road, I finally saw a light in the distance. It was the only gas station on that stretch of highway, so I pulled into the parking lot, hoping to find help. There was no one inside, but I spotted a payphone on the side of the building. I checked my wallet but had no change, only an old calling card my father had given me in case of emergency. I opened my door and ran to the phone. It wasn't covered, so I succumbed to the drenching rain as I tried to dial. My fingers shook uncontrollably as I struggled to remember the sequence of numbers: 800 calling card number, then the phone number I wanted to call, then my PIN number or 800 number, then PIN, then phone number. Every combination failed. It felt like that reoccurring nightmare when there is something in my locker I need desperately but I forget the combination. Finally, out of the corner of my eye, I saw a person walk inside the station. I dropped the receiver and ran in after him.

"Do you have a phone I can use?" I asked, not knowing who I was going to call. My mother couldn't do anything for me at this point, so I was contemplating 911 for the first time in my life. Still, I feared that interaction. What would I say when they asked me the problem? "It's raining and I need a ride home?"

"No, not for public. Phone outside, for you. You pay," said the attendant. "I know, I know. I tried, but I don't have any change, and I forgot my phone card numbers, and the rain is just …" I stopped to catch my breath. He wasn't looking at me anymore.

Just then, a state police car pulled into the station. It was my savior, like God had sent it just for me. The attendant left me and ran out into the rain, holding his coat over his head. I watched him pump gas into the cruiser, wondering what to say and how to ask for help. My mind was blank. I stood paralyzed as the attendant pulled the pump from the car, made change at the driver's window, and walked back into the station. The car drove away in what seemed to be slow motion. It was my savior … and it was gone.

I walked back to my car slowly—completely numb to the rain washing over me. I stared at the dark highway ahead and felt an intense sense of emptiness and isolation. I felt helpless and worthless and I cried as uncontrollably as the rain fell.

What would my fiancé think if he saw me like this? How could he love me? Would my mother be proud? How had I become so fragile and powerless? I was completely out of control. I put a self-help CD into the player in an effort to motivate myself but immediately ejected it. The sound of those words telling me I was divine and whole and enough made me sick because clearly, I was not. It had never been so clear.

When I turned on the radio, I heard a gentle woman's voice. It was a disc jockey named Delilah who takes calls from people with broken hearts and plays music to help them feel less alone. Her voice soothed me, and her stories and songs distracted me just enough to drive back into the abyss, into the unknown, and find my way home. I drove 30 mph and heard that whisper of grace each mile along the way saying, "Just a little bit further. Don't look back; just keep moving forward."

The trip took me twice as long as usual, and it was approaching midnight when I finally arrived home. I pulled into the parking lot, and rather than jump out of that car feeling liberated and vindicated, I dropped my head onto the steering wheel I was still clutching with white knuckles and thanked God for sending me grace to guide me home. My perception of myself had fallen to a new and embarrassing low. I could barely carry my overnight bag and my shame into my apartment. I would have to find a way to banish my anxiety for good or risk losing my fiancé, my job, and my future.

Unfortunately, I didn't know that the more I tried to control my anxiety and push it deeper below the surface, the stronger it would fight to resurface. That battle continued until I reached rock bottom, which was still on the horizon. Until then, I misdiagnosed my fleeting moments of calm as being cured. I didn't realize that my fears were metastasizing in the shadows, where they would either destroy me or guide me to redemption.

Chapter 18

The Light

"Anxiety does not empty tomorrow of its sorrows,
but only empties today of its strength."
—Charles Spurgeon

WHEN I FIRST MET GREG, the fog lifted temporarily only to reveal that the panic had moved in for good. Falling in love can be an effective distraction at first, but over time, a relationship only puts your fears and insecurities under a microscope, and eventually, your hidden secrets come to light.

As I saw my life falling into place, having found my husband and my first job, with love and a little money, I thought the pressure would be released and the anxiety would dissipate. But the opposite happened, and I struggled to understand why.

I thought my anxiety was caused by what was going on around me, not inside of me. If I could only control my environment, I wouldn't set it off and I would be normal again. My sister would always say, "There are a lot of rules with you." She didn't see the tightrope I was walking and the broken glass below. She didn't see the terrified little girl trying to impose rules that she thought kept her safe from all she could not control.

What I couldn't see was that those rules didn't apply anymore. The comfort they gave that child was an illusion, and I still couldn't see through it. I needed one of those stars in my constellation to shine a glimmer of light inside that box and bring some clarity.

I found that light in a hotel room in Park City, Utah, about six months after my wedding. I had a man who loved me, opportunities and adventures at my fingertips, and I chose to sit in a dark hotel room alone all day because I feared looking foolish and feeling vulnerable, both of which I characterized as failure.

We were on a ski trip with the Dartmouth Lawyers Club. Greg had raced on the US ski team, so I was looking forward to showing him off and maybe learning how to ski a little, even though everything about it terrified me. I agreed to take a lesson, which presented a myriad of challenges considering my anxiety.

First of all, wearing all the ski gear triggered intense claustrophobia for me. I felt completely immobile and trapped. Then there's the weather, which has always caused me anxiety. It's entirely out of your control and can be life-threatening, which for me was the definition of anxiety. But if you wait for perfect ski conditions in the mountains, which, for me, is fresh snow, blue skies, and no wind, you'll likely never ski.

Then there's the altitude (feeling oxygen-depleted is a sure road to a panic attack), my fear of heights, the threat of physical injury, and my phobia of being stuck without food. (I had provisions—as well as pills—in all of my pockets to prevent one of my "bonks.")

After my initial introduction to the ski instructor, I immediately revealed my general anxiety around skiing and risk of panic attacks through all phases of the lesson. And I reminded him over and over again. Being with someone who didn't know about my condition created a trap for me. Being without the ability to pull the ripcord and escape at any time created even more panic, so opening up to him relieved some pressure. And he was a safe stranger, not someone who could abandon or fire me.

When I told him I was afraid of the lift, he was very understanding, confirming it was common with inexperienced skiers. In a soothing voice, he talked me through each step and asked the lift operator to slow the chair down for me as it approached. It immediately calmed my nerves and quieted my mind.

Nonetheless, with adrenaline still coursing through my veins, my hands shook, and my legs grew weak as we soared high above the trails. The instructor distracted me with questions like, "What do you do for work? Why are you in Park City? Why are you learning how to ski as an adult?"

The first two questions made me feel confident telling him I was a lawyer and where I had studied in college. The third made me feel empowered, telling him of my accomplishments as an athlete and confidence in my ability to learn this new skill. To my surprise, the conversation diffused most of the anxiety, at least temporarily. I unclenched my hands, took a deep breath, and started to actually enjoy the beautiful view. And for just a moment, I forgot that I was ascending a mountain I had no idea how to get down.

The trails were wide open and just steep enough to keep me moving. My skis were in a pizza wedge much of the day, with my hands squeezing the life out of my poles and my feet cramping in rented ski boots. All the while, I was terrified that I would pick up too much speed, catch the edge of my ski, and career into another skier or a distant tree. Round and round we went for two hours with blue skies and warm temperatures. It was a perfect introduction.

On our last ride to the top of the beginner hill, I closed my eyes, felt the sun on my face, and a tear fall down my cheek. I also felt a twinge of pride—I had never in my life thought I would get on a chair lift, never mind find a moment of peace on one. It was just as big a mental challenge as skiing back down the mountain, and I was doing it.

After hearing of my success, Greg was eager to ski with me the next day. I was confused and slightly terrified. What was he thinking? He was an expert, and now he suddenly wanted to ski *together*. What did he think I had learned? I was in an awkward, hunched-over pizza wedge on a hill you could barely roll a ball down.

My confusion and self-consciousness turned into complete paralysis as I tried to understand how this would actually play out. How could one lesson bridge the chasm between our abilities? Where would our two trails converge?

As I raised questions and concerns, he dismissed them and just continued to beg me to come out and ski with him.

"Just try. Whatever you do is fine."

He thought a beautiful, sunny day and a kind, nonjudgmental husband would be enough to lure me back to the slopes. As I continued to refuse, I realized the depth of our disconnection around my anxiety. He was so comfortable in his equipment, in this environment, and in his own skin, he couldn't begin to understand me. Skiing was second nature, and anxiety was foreign to him. And for me, it was just the opposite.

The anxiety around skiing wasn't even the worst of it. I had far more anxiety around exposing myself and looking foolish in front of my husband, who I had been trying so hard to hide it from. That level of vulnerability terrified me. When that girl behind the curtain saw it, she slammed on the brakes. My walls were too high to allow such exposure.

The pain from the conflict raging inside felt like I was being torn apart at my seams. I wanted to ski. I wanted the adventure; I wanted to be fallible in front of him and have him love me anyway. I played it out in my mind's eye—the falling, the laughing, the trying, the allowing myself to appear imperfect. It felt like finally exhaling. I wanted to share that experience with him so badly. I'd seen that movie, and *that* girl is approachable and lovable. But my body tensed, and my mind recoiled at the thought of being judged and becoming even more replaceable.

So, I just stood there and watched him walk out of our hotel room, shaking his head. At first, I tried to justify my decision but soon realized that regardless of his inability to give me what I needed—empathy, comfort, digestible details, a plan that considered my skill level and mental frailties—I saw how the limitations I had placed on my life were affecting every aspect of it.

I paced around the bed and stopped at the window to watch the skaters circling the outdoor rink below. Their arms were spread wide as if they were trying to fly. They laughed and squealed with joy as their skates slipped out from under them. I put my forehead on the glass, wanting to feel what they felt. No one looked perfect; they just looked happy. The distance between me and them felt so much farther than just a few hundred feet. It was a chasm I feared I'd never cross.

My heart wanted to try and fail, to love completely and open myself up to feel all that came with it, the joy and the pain. I wanted to say, "Yes, I'll try, and if I look foolish, we'll laugh together. If I fall, you'll help me back up. If I'm scared, you'll comfort and reassure me. If I fail, you will still love me."

But in my mind, there was another voice, an intruder, who was pulling the strings.

So instead, I sat in that room paralyzed by her incessant questions:

"What if you panic and can't escape?"

"What if you aren't good enough?"

"What if you don't deserve what you have?"

"What if you are not lovable?"

"What if you are not strong enough?"

"What if you never find happiness?"

"What if you never reach your potential?"

"What if this anxious mess is all you'll ever be?"

"What if he saw the real you?"

"What if everyone saw everything you hide?"

Then she said, "Hopefully, he'll find a beautiful skier and leave us for her. Then we won't have to worry about his judgment and be afraid of him leaving anymore, and it will just be you and me again."

The choice was no longer my own. The little girl behind the curtain was working overtime, reinforcing those walls to keep me safe, physically and emotionally.

The walls of that hotel room now felt like more than just physical boundaries. It was as if someone flipped a switch, and suddenly, I could see the box I was in. These walls that were supposed to keep me safe had turned me into a prisoner. And in an instant, a light turned on that could never be dimmed again.

Renewal

I don't remember feeling the flowers and grass under my feet as I moved seamlessly through them, gliding and floating above a field of bursting colors without disruption. The sky glowed raspberry on one horizon, fading into lighter shades of pink higher in the sky until it was almost white directly above my head. It fell into a light shade of blue that grew deeper into a beautiful sapphire glow on the opposite horizon. It seemed there was more than one sun rising and setting.

And in a darkness that didn't dim the colors in the field, I saw millions of fireflies light up the space just above the blossoms in a light show so spectacular I stopped moving. My breath slowed, and I could feel my chest moving in slow motion as the air fell in and out. I couldn't look away.

After standing there for what seemed like more time than I was worthy of, birds began to sing, and I acknowledged that I had never felt as happy and at peace as I did at that moment. I exhaled fully, feeling every limb tingle with pure joy.

With every sense stimulated, I closed my mouth to inhale the perfume of the flowers and grasses but found nothing. No smell, no air. I was suddenly unable to breathe, as if there was no air left at all. As if I had used my share. Blood rushed to my head and adrenaline to my heart, making it quicken and pound through my chest. The light was growing faint, turning my images to black and white. The fireflies were suddenly gone, the singing turned to silence, and in a second, I saw the flowers dry up and shrivel on their stems.

I felt faint as suffocation set in. Suddenly, the air grew colder and seeped slowly into my chest. I found enough oxygen to think clearly for a moment. I paused, wondering if this would be my last breath. How long could I last if it was? How long would it be until my next?

I feared letting go of it and held on as long as I could until finally, I could hold it no more, and I exhaled. But it wasn't just that last breath that I exhaled; it was every breath I had ever taken. I felt every inch of my body releasing something—so much that it burned the back of my throat and became visible coming from my mouth, spreading across the field. It blew the dried petals off the flowers and into the air until only empty stems remained. I could feel the energy being sucked out of me until every bit was gone and I had nothing left.

I was exhausted, both physically and emotionally, but I was breathing again. Short, simple breaths. My hands rested on my knees, and my eyes focused on stems just below my feet. I moved to stand straight again and lost my footing. The only sound I heard was the crunching below my feet as they readjusted. As I looked toward the horizon, I saw the glow of another sun rising.

Chapter 19

Rock Bottom

*"Rock bottom became the solid foundation
on which I rebuilt my life."*
—J.K. Rowling

HONK! HOOONK! HONK!!! HOOONK!!!

I stared at the light as it turned green again, my foot planted firmly on the brake and my hands squeezing the steering wheel. Horns honked all around me but sounded a million miles away. The light had turned from red to green, back to red, and back to green again more times than I could recall. My rearview mirror reflected cars pulling out of my lane to go around me. I felt sharp stares piercing the side of my face as they passed, but I never took my eyes off the light.

Greg was on another sailing trip, and I hadn't left the house since I got home from work on Friday. Now Sunday evening, I was out of food and had no choice but to drive myself to the grocery store.

I hadn't driven alone this far from home in months. When I arrived at this traffic light, I had forgotten where I was going. I thought about aborting the trip altogether but couldn't remember how to get back home. As I drove further and further away from home, my mind was racing so fast that it went blank—suddenly and completely. I was already quite anxious when I left the house, knowing I would have a panic attack but confident I could fight through it. I never expected such a dense fog would roll in without warning.

As I struggled to identify my options, my breath grew so shallow that the car began spinning around me as my arms tingled with pins and needles. I could call 911 and ask them to send help, I could sit in the car and call my mother until the fog lifted, or I could take a left turn and reassess in a parking lot. Given I didn't know what to tell the 911 operator and was too ashamed to tell my mother I was lost within five miles of my house, I took a left turn. Then I saw it—the grocery store.

I parked and located the closest shopping cart, knowing I couldn't walk very far on my own. I grabbed hold of it to help steady my wobbly legs. As I wandered the aisles, the shelves seemed to teeter around me. I walked directly to the juice for some sugar to give me some clarity. I guzzled eight ounces, spilling some on my shirt from my hand shaking uncontrollably. When it provided no relief, I contemplated taking a pill. I convinced myself that the warning against operating heavy machinery included driving myself home, so I left it in my pocket. My only lifeline now was a shopping cart with only three functioning wheels that was barely holding me up. Knowing my time was limited, I chose the most important items on my grocery list, the ones that would get me through until Greg returned home.

At the register, my hands shook so intensely I handed my wallet to the cashier and asked her to process my credit card for me. I thought about how I was going to get myself home while she bagged my items. After hyperventilating for close to 30 minutes, I was physically exhausted, and my mind was completely empty. When she handed me my receipt, I just stared at it.

"Is there something wrong?" she asked.

"Could I leave my bags with you for a minute while I go back for something I forgot?" I asked, too ashamed to look up from the receipt and make eye contact.

"Sure," she said.

I took my empty shopping cart back to the magazine aisle, sat down on the lowest shelf, and cried. I was completely paralyzed. I tried to think through the next steps, one by one, but nothing made sense. I couldn't remember where I parked or my way home. I couldn't take a pill, and I couldn't call anyone and tell them I was stuck in the magazine aisle of the grocery store. It was too humiliating. So, I just sat and tried to breathe.

I didn't know how much time passed when I heard, "Are you sure I can't help you find anything?" Apparently, the clerk had already asked me this several times, but I didn't remember. I didn't even recognize him.

"No, thanks. I'm fine, really." I said, smiling with only my mouth. My eyes were lifeless.

"OK, well, we are closing in 10 minutes. So, let me know if there is anything I can do," he said.

"OK, thank you." I heard the words come out of my mouth, but it was as if I was listening to someone else talking. I stood up slowly, holding onto the shelf to stabilize myself, pretending to look at a magazine. I didn't recognize my hands as I watched them flip through the pages. Then I realized I couldn't even feel the pages. I inhaled deeply, contemplating my choices. I grabbed the empty shopping cart, walked through the sliding doors and down each row of the parking lot until I found my car.

As I turned the key, I prayed that the dense fog would recede just enough to see the breadcrumbs along the road leading me back home. And it did. I walked in the back door of our apartment empty-handed, my bags of food still at the grocery store. Having accomplished nothing but to confirm how small my world had become and completely exhausting myself in the process, I went straight to bed.

I never told Greg how bad things had gotten. Instead, I suffered in silence. I purposefully delayed my morning routine so I would miss the train and ask him for a ride to work. He worked from home, so he didn't find it a great inconvenience at first. I called him throughout the day from my office at the firm. I kept a strict routine. I avoided group lunches and board room meetings. I learned to hide my obsessive pulse-taking so I could do it even while sitting in a partner's office discussing matters. And by 3 p.m. each day, I feared a call from a partner with an assignment that would keep me later than expected—or maybe even all night. I knew that as a first-year associate I didn't control my life, the firm did, and it created another layer of anxiety that suffocated me.

Still, if I was lucky enough to make my train, the ride home had become unbearable. I needed an aisle seat to have an escape, which no one appreciated. Everyone wanted the aisle seat, so I just got nasty remarks and eye rolls when I stood up and allowed them into my row rather than sliding in toward the window. After a while, I never sat at all. I stood by the door and stared at the red lever, contemplating the white letters that read "Pull to Stop."

During each ride, it was just a matter of time until my heart skipped a beat, or several, then dropped into my stomach as I gasped for breath. The immediate thought of death shot adrenaline through my veins and sent me into a tailspin. I tried to stay standing as one hand immediately reached for my neck to confirm a pulse, while the other searched my briefcase for my phone to call my lifeline. Ironically, the only real danger I was in was being thrown off my feet as the train jostled around corners and along uneven rails without holding onto anything.

When Greg traveled for work, I was left alone to find my way to and from work. Those were the darkest times. While driving home from the commuter rail one night, I pulled over into the parking lot of a local gym to catch my breath. I looked through the window and watched the people exercising inside with envy. I had canceled my membership months ago.

I took out my pills and stared at the bottle illuminated by the streetlight. I was close enough to home to not worry about the caution against operating heavy machinery but feared taking it while I was alone. If something happened, there would be no one there to save me. Even though I had never had a bad reaction in the past, I didn't trust medication from one pill to the next. I put them back in my briefcase and picked up my cellphone. As I dialed my mother's number, a commercial came on the radio. It was a woman asking if I was suffering from anxiety or depression.

"Yes!" I answered aloud, as if she could hear me. I hung up the phone. It was Lucinda Basset from The Midwest Center for Anxiety and Depression. She assured me that I was not alone, and her CDs would provide relief. I was at rock bottom with nowhere to turn, and I was sent another lifeline.

They took a few weeks to arrive, but when they did, I devoured them. I listened to the CDs daily. Listening to the recordings of group therapy sessions was the first thing that gave me hope that I wasn't going crazy. The terrifying thoughts that occupied my brain were their thoughts, too, and they were just as terrified by them. Hearing the explicit detail of how their minds and bodies felt completely out of their control reassured me that I was not alone. I had never even shared my thoughts with a therapist, and here were all of these people sharing one after another after another. Every story meant something to me. I related to all of them in a different, yet deeply profound way. I wept for them, and then I wept for myself.

The CDs also armed me with tools I could use to avoid or deal with my next inevitable panic attack. They included a nightly meditation that guided me through deep breathing and a walk to a waterfall, as well as relaxation exercises to calm my body and slow down my racing mind. The techniques I learned were essential in starting my journey back from the bottom.

I learned that no physical symptom came without first having a thought. I started learning how to recognize my distorted and destructive thought patterns and unwind them before they spun out of control. I did workbook exercises that helped me understand my triggers, my fears, and ultimately, my disorder better than I ever had before.

While lifesaving at the time, I realized after several years that I was still deep in my box. These techniques helped me function again, and even explore the boundaries of my walls, but I was still afraid of the next panic attack and limiting my life to accommodate the anxiety. I was not living an empowered and fulfilled life—the life I was meant to live. The question then became, "Is my condition a life sentence and the box my prison, or could there actually be a way out?"

I was determined to find the answer.

Strange Cold Days

The black ripples rise into white-tipped peaks.
The water looks so cold.
Strong winds manipulate the current,
changing its direction without warning.
The sun is a welcome stranger
shedding perspective on the morning.
Oh! to be bold, and grab hold
and find warmth in this freeze
and a lift in this breeze.
But the birds have gone
taking their inspiration to a place
much brighter than here.
Even the trees, so stoic, have died.
On my cheeks are the freezing tears I've cried
and I am left here, alone.
Longing for a day when I see more than gray
and I feel more than cold.

Chapter 20

A Failure Worth Fighting For

*"We must be willing to let go of the life we've planned,
so as to have the life that is waiting for us."*
—Joseph Campbell

WHAT MADE THE MORNING of November 14 stand out was the kiss. It was not the typical goodbye kiss he gave me every morning. This was a long, deep kiss. Mouths open wide, tongues exploring each other slowly, his hand holding the back of my head. My knees buckled.

"If you kiss me like that every day, we'll be fine," I said, part plea, part threat.

The kiss was unexpected and out of character. It was an act of desperation. Our marriage wasn't working. It had been four years, but we only knew each other for five. When we fell in love, there were parts of each of us that the other had yet to discover. As these secrets found their way into the light, they took their toll on the relationship.

I didn't know exactly how a marriage should "work," given this was my first, but something was broken. He became emotionally unavailable and disinterested in intimacy. When pressed, he blamed it on my anxiety but otherwise declared that everything was fine from his perspective, his face expressionless. I wouldn't know the real reason for his distance until it was too late.

Over the last year, I shifted my focus to having children, hoping to find something to bond over, but found myself reminding him regularly that in order to conceive a child, we would actually need to have intercourse. His indifference seeded resentment that over time became misery and fear. My interest in having a child then shifted from something to bond over to something to bond with—something to love that would respond and love me back. And as a result, my interest in him proportionately diminished.

Was this it? We were sitting in a new home on a new couch with a sweet dog and absolutely nothing to say to each other. My box had never looked more perfect, and it disguised the discontent building inside.

He trivialized my fears and grew frustrated by my anxiety. His only advice was to "feed the good dog." That was easier said than done when my bad dog had already eaten my good dog for breakfast. He believed it shouldn't exist and so pretended it didn't, which only created more anxiety for me. As a result, I was forced to deal with my anxiety alone and build more walls to hide it.

By hiding parts of myself that he didn't understand or approve of, I felt unseen and silenced. He didn't love who I actually was, which in turn meant that I, as is, with anxiety, was unlovable. And the more I felt his love was conditional, the more I resented him for it.

As a result, my marriage caused more anxiety because there was no way out, no safe place to retreat. I was in a relationship that had no space or tolerance for it. I know now that once you give your anxiety a voice, it quiets down; once you shine a light on it, it dissipates. But ignoring it and pushing it further underground expands and empowers it. The Wizard does not want to be ignored.

During our divorce proceedings, Greg said, "Your anxiety was like a third person in this relationship."

Yes. One that was clearly underappreciated by you, I thought.

Relationships can either force you further into your box or empower you to find your way out. They can be a potent source of strength, balance, and hope, or they can extinguish all three.

A few weeks before our wedding, we met with Nigel, the minister that would marry us. He seemed to be hundreds of years old, both in his appearance and his wisdom.

Nigel's office was a claustrophobic fire hazard, to say the least. It had room for one person and maybe their tiny visitor. I walked in after Nigel, wondering how my fiancé would fit. Once we all sat down, I would have to crawl over a desk or my fiancé's lap to reach the door.

After brief introductions, Nigel turned to my fiancé and asked, "Why do you love her?" When he was done answering the question, I completely broke down.

"Why are you crying?" Nigel asked. I stayed silent, reaching for a tissue. "Are these tears of joy?"

"No," I whispered.

"So then where are they coming from, dear?"

"I don't know," I replied, wiping tears from my eyes and wanting desperately to escape. The pain in my chest was so fierce it felt ignitable. One spark and that tiny room would have lit it up like a Roman candle.

I was trapped in that tiny room with those words lingering in the air. I tried to swat them away like flies as I grabbed more tissues off the desk.

"Well, maybe you should explore that, my dear," the minister replied slowly while his eyes burned holes in my forehead. I couldn't look up from the tissue I was tearing into small pieces in my lap. I felt as if he could see right into my soul.

While I didn't know why I was crying, I could feel the depth of the well from which those tears flowed and knew we didn't have that kind of time. The wedding was in just three weeks.

I know now that I felt broken, defective. I felt fundamentally unlovable. That is a difficult place from which to build a deep connection, a loving relationship, and a lifelong partnership. I was looking at a man who loved me from behind very high walls. It was my burden to bear as I moved through the motions of a wedding and a marriage.

Before that kiss, we'd struggled through months of couples therapy. I wanted desperately for him to come out of the shadows and engage, to show some vulnerability, some desperation in the face of losing me and this life we had together. He had been unmoved by my claims of disconnection and only disengaged more when I challenged him. He sat in the therapist's chair completely comfortable, exuding confidence in the relationship and responding robotically to questions with "Yes, I do," or "No, never," and "That's normal for married couples."

Meanwhile, my sweaty hands shook, and my right knee bounced uncontrollably. I cried while disclosing my deepest frustrations, giving example after example of a lack of an intimate relationship. The therapist struggled to bridge the chasm between us that I felt so deeply and he was choosing to ignore. I needed to know why, but he wouldn't break. Acknowledging the disconnection would mean acknowledging my pain, the reality of his marriage unraveling, and his responsibility in both.

Feeling suffocated by the lack of progress, I decided separation was the next step. It would be my final attempt at making him realize the gravity of the situation. I planned to wait until after the holidays as a final token of compassion. In the meantime, days passed without a word spoken. Weeks passed without eye contact. He started sleeping in the guest room. Even the dog was confused. Then suddenly, it was December 23.

Intent on one last workout before my family arrived, I filled a water bottle and made my way to the car. Still in the garage, I sat in the driver's seat with the keys in my lap, my body limp. Tears streamed down my face as I thought about the last three years—our first encounter, the wedding, the secrets, and the news I was dreading delivering. I was still searching for what went wrong, and time was running out. I guess it didn't matter anymore. Separation would just be a physical expression of what already existed emotionally.

To stay would mean giving up any hope of ever having a meaningful and fulfilling relationship with my husband. It would mean being complicit in my own misery and ultimately his. It would also mean losing myself in the process forever. Regardless of the obvious and cliché admission of failure the world would see in a divorce, this failure was one worth fighting for.

Driving to the gym, I wondered what would happen next. I would ask him to move out, and then what? It was imperative and yet, unimaginable, paralyzing even. It was like stepping into a dark tunnel with no guarantee there was an opening at the other end. And if there was, how far did I need to go to reach it, and where would it lead?

I stopped at a red light and pulled down the visor to shade my eyes from the blinding December sun. With one hand still off the wheel, I felt a sudden explosion in the back of the car, and everything faded to black.

The sound of someone banging on my window brought me back as sirens echoed in the distance. A young man was pacing outside the car with blood on his face and shirt. His lips were moving, but I couldn't hear him. My head pounded. Panic set in as my heart raced uncontrollably. I felt the adrenaline pulsing through my veins.

I pulled the door handle and fell out of the car to the ground. The young man rushed over to help, looking relieved to see me alive. "Are you OK?" he asked breathlessly, over and over again. I staggered in the road, still wondering what happened as cars slowly drove past, staring at the wreckage. Finally, a man emerged from an ambulance and guided me to the side of the road. He asked what I remembered and how I felt while the young man interjected, "I couldn't see. I couldn't see her car in the sun."

"I don't know. I don't feel right. My heart is racing and my head. Oh God, my head!" I pulled my hand from the wet, sticky area that had smashed the windshield and found blood all over it.

Lying on a stretcher in the back of the ambulance, the paramedic checked vitals and gave me a valium. I felt a strange heat building in my stomach and suddenly wondered if I could be pregnant. I prayed all the way to the hospital that there was a baby inside me that was safe and sound and that news of the accident and the baby would finally resuscitate my husband.

After tests and time, the doctor confirmed there was a concussion but no baby. As I lay on the hospital bed listening to the diagnosis, Greg stood there emotionless. He seemed completely unaffected by yet another possibility of losing me. I suddenly wished it had been worse. Maybe then he would have been shocked enough to realize I could have died, and he couldn't imagine the thought of living without me. I stared at him, awaiting his response.

"Ready to go?" he said, finally making eye contact.

It was excruciating. I looked away, my eyes burning as they filled with tears.

I wished it had been worse.

Mad Winds

When the sea is churned
by winds from the northeast
and the hungry gulls come to feast.

When the moon rises in the east
setting hearts afire and horizons aglow...

that's when I'll know...
it's time to go.

Chapter 21

The Choice

"And the day came when the risk to remain
tight in a bud was more painful
than the risk it took to blossom."
—Anais Nin

"OPEN YOUR EYES and look around you. Look at where you've ended up and how different that is from what you intended." The voice inside my head grew louder as my awareness of the box grew stronger. The limitations I had placed on my life were endless and reflected back at me in every brick. I was not who I wanted to be, nor was I living the life I had dreamed of, or that I knew was possible.

In protecting myself from rejection and abandonment, I was more alone than ever. In protecting myself from failure, I felt unfulfilled. In protecting myself from death, I was terrified of living.

To the world, the box I had created looked picture perfect—they couldn't see I was unraveling inside. I was more anxious than ever because while I was drowning, I knew they couldn't even see the water. No one would believe me or know how to help. From the outside looking in, there was nothing to fix.

My determination to still function at a high level meant hiding exactly what I needed them to see if I was going to get the help I needed. My anxiety was no longer just a dark, ominous cloud of potential panic that followed me everywhere I went. Its tentacles had found their way into the deepest places within me, affecting my life in overt as well as subtle and subversive ways.

I had a choice. I could resign myself to the diagnosis, concede to my pre-disposition to a life riddled with anxiety and blame it on my environment and genetics. I could stay in the box and live a life that looked and sounded perfect to everyone but me. I could white-knuckle it, taking pills to hide the panic percolating just below the surface. I could continue to retreat, sacrificing connection with my husband and family. I could have children to love and care for, and possibly fill the voids I had created but more likely pass on the anxiety I carried.

I could work obscenely long hours at my law firm, arriving home in time to kiss my children goodnight, work a few more hours and then climb into bed after my husband fell asleep. I could wake up and do it all again, knowing my husband would pretend everything is fine for as long as I am willing to be complicit in the charade. I could pray that in living this lie, my anxiety would not intensify. And I could be destroyed by that unanswered prayer, day after day after day.

Or I could imagine living my life from that authentic place inside of me that, until now, was losing the battle to that little girl. I could feel truly connected and fulfilled by my relationships. I could be exhilarated by new adventures and calm in my own body. I could live an intentional life where my mind was my benevolent friend, not my vengeful enemy.

This was not an exercise in "finding my purpose" or "calling." This was about the basic needs for which we are all hardwired—love, connection, fulfillment, and peace. I knew this life could not ever exist for me in the box. Now that the light was on, there was no going back.

To find my way out, I would need to understand how I got there. My journey had always been rooted in fear. Fear of things that caused me anxiety was worse than fear of the anxiety itself. Fear of living and fear of dying. There were years when I forgot it was walking quietly beside me and years when it sat on my chest, keeping me flat on my back.

Even though the walls were becoming clear, and I knew anxiety was the mortar holding the bricks together, I didn't know how or why I had constructed them. I had unknowingly given up all control of my life to that little girl, but she was still behind the curtain. I didn't know she existed, so I couldn't imagine a way out.

Nonetheless, the need to find a way came from a place deep inside. It called to me so strongly that I couldn't ignore it anymore. I had to find out what was holding me back so I could find what was waiting for me on the other side of those walls.

I had no evidence or examples of people who were afflicted and found their way out. The CDs helped me cope, and the self-help books provided a general sense of hope. Therapy was a place to throw some of my broken pieces on the table to examine, but none of them seemed to fit together. I would have to forge my own path and find my own way.

As I contemplated my choice, I remembered preparing for the final state track meet just before high school graduation. One of my best friends and I drove 45 minutes to the beach to run in the sand and mentally prepare for the upcoming (and potentially final) competition of our high school careers. After our run, we walked out to the end of a jetty and sat on the rocks. Our talk led us beyond the meet as we imagined where our college years would take us, as she, too, was traveling far from home to attend university. We talked about what had led us to where we were and how we would know the right choices to make in the future.

I looked at the river on one side of the jetty and the ocean on the other. I knew exactly where that river would lead. It was calm and predictable. But it was also narrow and shallow, limited in what it could accommodate and provide. On the other side, the ocean was vast and violent at times, smashing against the rocks as the waves rolled in. It was deceptively deep, with no way of knowing what was under the surface. The possibilities were endless, but so were the perils.

With a lot of hope and a little trepidation, we bowed our heads and prayed together, knowing that our futures might present more challenges than our last four years:

> "Dear God, we are so thankful for the opportunities you have bestowed on us. We know we will always have the choice to jump into the river or the ocean. The safe choice and the challenging one. There will always be a right and a wrong answer. Grant us the courage to choose what is right, to choose what challenges us, to choose what might be unpopular, to choose what will break our heart open, stir our spirit and strengthen our resolve."

I thought of that jetty often during the years that passed, and I drew on that prayer. I knew in the ocean I would be immersed in pain and panic, but I could also be buoyed by its promise and possibility.

As I considered leaving the box and heading out into the open ocean that lay on the outside of those walls, I felt a paradigm shift in my soul. I became more afraid of not living than I was of dying. Living an unexamined and unfulfilled life suddenly felt like a death sentence.

So, I asked myself,

"Will I regret my decision if I stay?"

"I know I am far from fearless, but do I have the courage to find my way out?"

"Is it worth the pain and vulnerability of facing my greatest fears on that journey?"

"Is it worth risking every ounce of comfort, safety, and security I have in my box, real or imagined, with no certainty of the outcome?"

And the answer was yes.

The answer is always yes.

Part 3

FINDING MY WAY OUT

Chapter 22

The Perfectionist

"You wouldn't worry so much about what
others think of you if you realized
how seldom they do."
—Eleanor Roosevelt

"OTHER THAN THOSE PEOPLE who have suffered greatly because of their perfectionism or the perfectionism of a loved one, the average person has very little understanding of how destructive perfectionism can be," says Dr. Gordon Flett, a psychologist at York University. Psychologist Thomas S. Greenspon explains, "Perfectionistic people typically believe that they can never be good enough, that mistakes are signs of personal flaws, and that the only route to acceptability as a person is to be perfect. Often, this turmoil can be difficult for others to see or even for the perfectionist to acknowledge, as those who suffer often work diligently to maintain a cohesive image of accomplishment and well-being."[17]

In looking at the walls I'd built, the first thing I noticed was how perfectly they had been constructed. I knew then that I needed to take a closer look at my perfectionism, the benefits I thought it would provide, and how it had become such a destructive force in my life. Where did the entanglement begin?

It began early, in the trenches of the chaos. I danced on the head of a pin so I wouldn't trigger my mother's rage. I made my bed, I cleaned my room, helped cook, set the table, and I even ate the pancakes she accidentally smothered in Dawn dishwashing detergent instead of maple syrup. She was in a tirade that I couldn't chance escalating by complaining. The bubbles floating from my lips and nostrils as I chewed and cried ultimately gave me away. She eventually apologized and tore the plate from the table to erase the mistake.

From the outside, I was smart and disciplined, and a very hard worker. I was always willing to sacrifice the fun of childhood for a grade or performance that would prove I was perfect, because on the inside, my self-worth and lovability were teetering in the balance.

But that was the textbook explanation. It felt more fiery and almost vengeful now. Why was I still working on it as an adult, long after the chaos had calmed and love was evident? When did that shift happen, and what was behind it? What lit that flame?

I followed the breadcrumbs—the relationships, the conversations, the people I longed to connect with the most. They led me back to the night before my first day of high school.

"Well, what do you think?" I asked with butterflies in my stomach.

I stood in front of my mother wearing the outfit I'd been planning since the fireworks crackled on the 4th of July.

"No one is looking at you," she said, barely looking up from her wine glass. My stomach churned, killing all the butterflies in an instant. She took a drag from her cigarette and stared blankly out the window as if I'd left the room.

I looked down at my skirt and the low-slung belt, the matching slouchy socks and sweater. The importance of this outfit on my high school career was lost on her. Or maybe not. Maybe she knew exactly how important it was to me and used her words to break me before anyone else could.

I knew that her experience in high school was barely tolerable, so maybe she had already lived this exact moment herself and been crushed under its weight. Her father died when she was just two years old, and her mother couldn't afford new clothes for her fourth child's first day of high school. Maybe she wore the same clothes her older sister had worn just two years earlier, and she was mortified that someone might notice. Maybe she was telling me to expect nothing on that first day of high school and not be disappointed when nothing was exactly what I got because that was *her* experience.

I will never know if this was said out of anger because her wounds were still open or if she was trying to save me from what she believed was inevitable disappointment. She felt both the pain of being invisible to those looking for the popular, pretty girls and the pain of being *too* visible to those looking for someone to taunt and jeer. In this moment, I felt invisible to the person I wanted to see me the most.

Her response not only confirmed that I wasn't special, but that I didn't matter. No one cared who I was, much less what I was wearing. I heard, "No matter what you wear, it can't change who you are," and who I was wasn't good enough.

That short response was her way of telling me that I was unworthy of love without actually having to say the words. Our dysfunctional relationship suddenly made sense. This was the highly anticipated confirmation of her disdain given on the eve of my first day of high school. The timing could not have been worse, and I hated her for it.

It was that teenage hate. That awful word that we use when we first feel rage at such a young age. My rage came from years of longing to be seen and heard, to be considered, consoled, or even celebrated. To be loved. I hated her for saying those words, and I hated myself for being a daughter unworthy of the attention of a stranger, much less my own mother.

When you are told you are less than and not enough, you see the world through a tainted lens and hear things in a different key. Your heart is so empty that it restricts your ability to love and feel loved, even your ability to see and hear things with compassion or clarity. Just like "You will never be the pretty one," it played over and over in my head like a hammer hitting nails into those pretty, perfect walls I was building.

I believed that if it shined brightly enough, she would *have* to see me. If I were perfect, she would have no choice but to see that I deserved attention, and in turn, she would regret her decision. And that's when the switch flipped from wanting her love to wanting to make her regret it. My perfectionism wasn't keeping the peace anymore; it was disrupting it.

Fortunately, my perfectionism was never overtly self-destructive, but quite the opposite. If I needed to earn love, I was ready to work extremely hard for it. I was not going quietly into the invisible, lonely existence my mother's comment foreshadowed. And I received enough positive reinforcement to perpetuate it. This is why so many high-performing, seemingly well-adjusted, over-achievers are anxious.

It first became destructive in my relationships. It was a never-ending, unwinnable battle. The more I sought perfection to win acceptance and love, the greater the distance grew between me and those from whom I sought it. While perfection may be attractive on a superficial level or envied by strangers, it doesn't create deep connection. My perfectionism didn't increase my intimacy; it increased my isolation.

Why? Because perfection isn't warm and welcoming. It isn't authentic and vulnerable. People view it as attention-seeking, which feels disingenuous, and it causes their own feelings of inadequacy to surface, all of which create barriers rather than bridges. And if they do view you as perfect, then you are on a pedestal—all by yourself.

People are attracted to vulnerability, flaws, and shared struggles because we can all relate to that. It's acknowledging those imperfections that moves them to open their arms and welcome you in. It's sharing your greatest fears over coffee that creates the deepest bonds. I would need to get comfortable with messy if I was going to find the connection I longed for.

My perfectionism also became destructive when it forced me to hide my anxiety from others as it worsened. I blamed my anxiety on being less than perfect in some way—my body, my thoughts, my insecurities, my fears. When in reality, my anxiety worsened because I couldn't acknowledge my imperfections and reframe them as my unique qualities. My "imperfections" became intolerable, increasing my anxiety and perpetuating my perfectionism. And round and round it went—the battle with myself—creating a vicious cycle.

Looking back to better understand my walls, I realize that my perfectionist behaviors accounted for countless bricks. From when all I wanted was to be seen, until all I wanted was to hide.

In hindsight, I like to think what my mother was trying to do or would have done if she had the ability at the time, was to free me from the pressure that all eyes would be on me and the scrutiny that comes with that. Stepping into high school hallways for the first time can be terrifying. Now, with more time and awareness, I hear that same sentence as inspiration instead of an insult.

"Wear whatever you want to wear. My opinion isn't important, only yours is. Be whoever you want to be—that choice is uniquely yours. You are already more amazing than I could have imagined.

Don't look to me or anyone else for approval. And even though they may be, just keep telling yourself, 'No one is looking at me.'"

Reframing the story would give me permission to look and feel exactly as I was and to love every part of it. Freedom from the judgment and pressure of critical eyes. Those eyes that mold you over time into something you never intended—without your consent—until you become what you believe they want to see.

We all deserve to feel what happens when we dismiss our critics as unworthy to collaborate in our journey. We all have an authentic path that is only compromised when we feel the lights of an uninvited audience. Their scrutiny doesn't light our way; it's illuminated by the light that shines from within.

Once in this state, I no longer sought the acceptance of others, even my mother, because the only acceptance I needed was my own. And once that version of myself was revealed, the walls of perfectionism came crashing down. I was free to be exactly who I was and, through that, end the battle. Empowered by this new mindset, I was ready to set out on my journey with a new level of understanding and compassion for all my broken and beautiful pieces. As more lines were drawn between the stars, they pointed me to the next step on my journey, giving me the courage to face the unknown challenges that lay ahead.

Chapter 23

The Snowflake

"Everything is perfect until we compare it to something else."
—Me

I REMEMBER WATCHING the snow fall outside my window as I contemplated my marriage ending. I was so defined by that perfect picture—the husband, the house, the golden retriever, the fertility monitor. It was a picture I'd dreamed of my entire anxious life. It was all supposed to erase my anxious thoughts and protect me from myself.

What would I be left with if it all came crashing down? Where would I find protection if I completely exposed myself? How would I define myself on the other side? How would others define me? Would they assume it was my anxiety or perfectionism that caused the rift, the lack of intimacy, and the ultimate demise of the union? Is that how I would be defined, by my mistakes and mental health issues? Could I really let go of the picture, the illusion of protection and perfection? Couldn't I just stay, finding ways to cope and blending in with the other "not so happy" couples that appeared to be keeping it all together?

I was 34 years old and couldn't help but compare myself to my friends who were upsizing everything to make space for their growing families, the women at church with their new babies, and the women at my firm on track to becoming partners. There were no cracks in their armor, no visible weaknesses threatening the dream. They were full steam ahead while I was coming off the tracks. Was I actually derailing my life by leaving my marriage? Most days, just thinking about letting go of it felt so raw and terrifying, I wasn't sure I would survive it. It required me to have faith in something I didn't know actually existed yet. It required that I trust there was something better on the other side of my walls, and in order to do that, I needed to believe in myself and the difficult decisions I'd have to make along the way.

My mind wandered to the miracle of the snowflakes and what they represent—each one different from the next. Each is uniquely beautiful, intricate, and perfect in its own way.

Then I imagined one snowflake seeing another and feeling less than or not good enough, longing to look and feel like another. Melting itself down to alter its angles, lose some crystals, reducing its water content, and changing its texture until it looked and felt exactly like the one it thought was better. A profound sadness washed over me as I imagined that snowflake would never realize it was perfect all along in its uniqueness and would be lost forever. And there would never be another one like it.

Everything is perfect until we compare it to something else.

That lingered in the back of my mind as I became engrossed in each flake. I realized at that moment that the source of so much of my anxiety, fear, and shame through the years could be directly linked to comparing myself to others.

Value is defined as "the importance, worth, or usefulness of something." I learned the hard way that when I look outside myself to determine my value or answer the question, "Am I enough?" I am playing a dangerous, unwinnable game of comparison.

Like snowflakes, we are all created with a divine individuality. I lost sight of that when I compared myself to others and allowed my ego to take over and talk me into a senseless competition. And I was encouraged by a society that critiques and discourages differences instead of celebrating and cultivating them.

Psychiatrists describe this constant comparison as "monkey brain." This type of behavior is common among primates, even chickens. But only humans have the level of consciousness to acknowledge what we are doing, realize its destructive nature, and change our behavior.

But it takes practice because we are taught to compare ourselves from a very young age. The ego grows stronger as it perpetuates itself, cutting those grooves so deep they are difficult to redirect.

For years, rather than seeing myself as a diamond, celebrating the unique facets that reflect and shine my light, I filed them down to a smooth, perfectly dull surface that reflected only insecurity. I didn't realize I was stripping away what made me interesting, covering up the scars that told my story and sanitizing my journey. By chasing after images of perfection and illusions of happiness I saw outside myself, I lost myself in a sea of snowflakes.

It would only be when I had the courage to step out and break my heart open, expose what felt like weakness, bleed my story onto the page, and shine a light in my dark places … only when I was brave enough to see my differences as gifts and my individuality as divine, that I would find my path to freedom. A freedom from anxiety that would bear gifts of connection and love beyond my wildest dreams.

I meditated on that snowflake to find perspective and strength. I could see every crystal as a part of me, reflecting how I had grown and how my unique journey had affected me over time. Each branch represented the paths I had taken, not all connected to each other necessarily, but connected by the center—by me. A perfect web of interlaced experiences reflected by a beautiful, divinely unique creature. There can be no comparing what is authentic. In that, there is no judgment. There is no better or worse, strong or weak, crazy or sane, pretty or ugly; only different. And it is all perfect.

Chapter 24

The Prisoners

"I saw the angel in the marble and carved
until I set him free."
—Michelangelo

MICHELANGELO IS BEST known for his fresco painted on the ceiling of the Sistine Chapel and his sculpture *David*. Although I have been blessed to see both, my favorite Michelangelo work is *The Prisoners*—a group of unfinished sculptures in the Galleria dell'Accademia in Florence. What draws me in is not their unfinished state, but what those extra pieces of marble represent and what hides beneath them.

Michelangelo described his work as a sculptor as liberating the forms imprisoned in the marble. "Every block of stone has a statue inside it, and it is the task of the sculptor to discover it," he said. We now know that he deliberately left *The Prisoners* incomplete. He meant for these figures emerging from blocks of marble to symbolize humankind's struggle to free the spirit from the matter or the soul being burdened by the flesh.[18]

When I hear "matter" and "flesh," I often think of only the body, but our mind can't be overlooked when considering these shackles. The flesh can encompass any human derivative, your body *or* your mind. Our mind is not our spirit or soul, just as we are not our thoughts. Which is why I identify so strongly with these figures more than the ideal portrayed by the *David* or the salvation promised by the ceiling of the Sistine Chapel.

The Prisoners are struggles in progress. Not struggling to find their form, but struggling to be free of it, whether that means physically or mentally.

I always thought *David* was simply the ideal, a perfect body portrayed in this innocent yet powerful figure. But given the metaphor of *The Prisoners*, perhaps Michelangelo intended more than that. Perhaps the *David*, in his naked, most vulnerable physical state, is supposed to represent the ideal of the spirit and soul finally freeing itself of the shackles of form and matter. So, we exalt it on a pedestal.

In contrast, *The Prisoners* line the hallway that leads to the *David*. They have been placed along the path that leads to the pedestal, the ultimate goal—enlightenment, redemption, and salvation. This metaphor unlocked something inside me as I continued on my journey out of the box.

We are all prisoners of something. One day, we wake up and realize the walls are closing in around us, and we feel the conflict deep within our souls. *The Prisoners* are far more representative of our daily, human struggle. The constant work of peeling back the layers and chipping away at the excess marble to expose our vulnerability and reveal the authentic truth that lies beneath it. This stone weighs us down, hides our insecurities, and holds us back from freeing our spirit to live in its own authentic light.

I think the question is not *are* we prisoners, but what are we prisoners *of?* From what do we need to free ourselves? As I picture myself inside a block of marble, I see the parts I've allowed the world to see. And I see the pieces that have been chipped away or worn down to expose different parts with and without my consent. Identifying the pieces that still remain, hiding my most painful parts and my deepest secrets point me to the next part of my journey.

Somewhere under all those extra pounds, whether physical or mental, a version of myself was waiting to be revealed. What was holding me back? My fear of exposure, judgment, confirmation that I was not enough or unworthy of love? Or maybe it was what Marianne Williamson so insightfully quoted in *A Return to Love* from *A Course in Miracles*: "Our deepest fear is not that we are inadequate. Our deepest fear is that we are powerful beyond measure. It is our light, not our darkness that most frightens us."

I knew that somewhere within that marble was an authentic spirit I could hear calling me—one that I longed to set free. The version of me that falls asleep after judgment and wakes up before fear.

I had to ask myself, "Where is the plaque that has built up between me and the truest expression of myself? What are the barriers I've built between myself and the relationships I desired? What will it take to identify the excess marble and chip away at it? What tools will I need? What will it take to expose those places that were never accessible before?"

I would have to do it one chip at a time, not knowing what it would reveal, only having the courage to keep chipping without attachment to what I was leaving behind on the sculptor's floor, but confident that it no longer served me.

The Real Questions

What if I told you my scariest thoughts
and shared my biggest fears?
Would you tell me yours
or stand behind your curtain of shame and judge me?

What if I told you how much I need you,
how much I truly love you?
Would you embrace it and reciprocate?
Could you hold the whole of my humanity
or would the weight of it crush you?
Would your heart break
in the face of my blood-red tears?
Would my vulnerability shut you down even further
or break you wide open?

Why does your embrace hover just beyond my bones
and your kiss float gently by my cheek?
Why won't you meet me

in the midst of my despair?
Don't you feel it too?
Don't you long for my touch,
for the sound of my voice,
for the scent of my skin that brings you back
to that place of comfort and peace?

Am I counting touches and kisses,
keeping irrelevant score
when there is something you aren't telling me,
something that's so much more?

Chapter 25

The Decision

*"[T]he world's greatest lie...is this: that at a
certain point in our lives, we lose control of
what's happening to us, and our lives become
controlled by fate."*
—Paolo Coelho

WHEN THE ALARM went off at 8 a.m. on December 26, he was already
out of bed and brushing his teeth in the master bathroom. After
months of sleeping apart, he and the dog were forced back into my
bedroom while my family occupied the guest rooms over the holiday.

The car accident had highlighted my mortality in a way that made
time more precious than ever. Combined with his callous response, I
was unable to contain my decision for as long as I'd planned to.

"I want a divorce," I said, skipping right over a separation. I assumed
he would be devastated, and I'd backpedal to a trial separation to meet

him in the middle. I intended to wait until after the "holidays" but couldn't imagine another week alone with him in silence, listening only to the clock ticking down to midnight on December 31. So, I downgraded New Year's from a holiday to a mere celebration, like a birthday, and with complete disregard for him and my family down the hall, lobbed a grenade into the bathroom and watched it roll around the feet of a man unable to save himself. He spit out the toothpaste and looked at me. He was crying—finally.

"What?!" he exclaimed. "I don't even know how to undo all of this," he said angrily, waving at the closet and furniture.

"Neither do I, but I don't care. That's not a reason to stay together like this. People have unraveled far more complicated situations, so I'm sure we'll figure it out. You deserve more than this. You deserve to be really loved."

"You don't love me?"

"Of course, I love you, but I don't feel *in love*. Not anymore. And you certainly don't act like you're in love with me. We aren't getting anywhere in therapy, and we both deserve more." My response was pragmatic, but I felt as if I was sinking in quicksand. There was a sense of relief that the struggle was finally over, but there was also a sense of terror. I knew I was taking a big step into that terrifying tunnel, and there was no turning back.

"Once you do this, it's over. There is no going back," he said, confirming what I already knew. If he was incapable of recognizing this sinking ship, he wasn't going to throw me a lifeline now. I was going down alone.

It was as if he was pointing to the tunnel I would walk into alone with no light at the end and asking, "I'm not going in there after you. Are you sure this is really what you want?" How could I be sure? I was terrified of leaving even though I knew on a deep level that this wasn't going to work unless he cracked himself open and exposed as much as I had. I was still desperate for him to fight for me and us by doing just that—showing some sign of vulnerability and passion. After weeks of discussions, the tears washed away any hope of that happening, and he moved out.

Weeks went by, and I still waited for a call. I stood paralyzed in front of that tunnel, holding out hope he'd save me from it. When I heard nothing, I engaged a lawyer to file for divorce. It would be simple—no children, no assets, no evidence that it ever happened, except the new designation of "divorced" as my marital status and a broken heart.

We put the house up for sale and the process moved slowly. Going home every night to the memories and questions that lingered in the air was painful and exhausting. I pictured my life after the house sold in a one-bedroom apartment with a single lightbulb hanging from the ceiling over a hot plate, the only heat I'd have. I'd sit on a crate stirring soup, huddled under a blanket to stay warm, counting the flies on the walls and the minutes till bedtime, surrounded by cats to comfort me.

The bar next to my office in the city became a far more palatable refuge for contemplation. Perched on my barstool, wine in hand, the questions seemed endless: *Divorced at 35, what would people think? How would I convince them this was a success, not a failure? How would I redefine myself? What would I learn from this? How would I keep my heart open to trying again? How would I trust someone? Are there single men at this age? Where would I live?*

There was a regular stream of commuters who came into the bar for a drink while they waited for their train to leave the city. When I wasn't dissecting my divorce, I watched other people having fun and acting like everything was normal. It was a welcome distraction and kept my hope of a future intact, no matter how unimaginable it seemed.

One night, a familiar face walked in. We went to school together and knew the same people, but I couldn't remember ever actually

speaking to him. He came right over and sat down. After initial rein-
troductions, his questions began.

"Married?"

I hesitated. "Yes."

"Kids?"

"No. Nope. None. A dog. That's as far as I got. Yeah. A dog. I can
see *you're* married." I deflected, glaring at his ring. "Kids?"

"Yeah!" he shouted, twisting his wedding ring, as if pulled from a
daze. "Three, actually." He threw his shoulders back and puffed out
his chest with a look of fear on his face like a deer in the headlights.
Then he dropped his head to stretch out his neck as if the thought
of them pained him. "Irish Catholic, what can I say?" he said with
a half-smile as if it had been totally out of his control and a genetic
burden he had to bear.

He suddenly felt safe to me. Married with three kids, common
friends and backgrounds, someone I could confide in. Someone completely disinterested in me romantically or otherwise. No pickup lines,
no innuendos, no subtle advances. Just a sweet smile and a generous
ear.

"Actually, I just filed for divorce," I revealed with an immediate sip
of wine to follow. Then another sip before I said, "It was my idea. I
left him." Sip. "Crazy, right?"

I hadn't told anyone outside of my family and the realtor until
now. It was a relief to let the words spray across the bar like confetti.

"I had to. It just wasn't right ... at all. He was fine; there was no
cheating, no beating, no nothing. It just wasn't right, and I knew that,
deep inside. I don't want to live like that. I want more for myself, and
he deserves more, too. I did it in part because I love him as a person.
In part because I couldn't stand who I had become. There are a lot of
parts, but in the end, I really feel confident in my decision and view

it as a success, not a failure. Unfortunately, I know everyone will see it as a *huge* failure.

"The easy thing would have been to stay and have children and focus on them while trying to forget what it feels like to be loved and desired and touched and intimately connected to another human being. And my children would have seen it and felt it. He would have been a great father, but they would never have seen a great husband or a great wife, a great marriage. That was too much for me to lose. Ironically, it would have been my greatest failure."

There it was. Off my chest and in the world as my dogma. I said it—out loud—and it felt amazing. Cracking myself open to someone I hardly knew felt effortless. He had no preconceived notions, no prior knowledge or judgment.

"I think it's amazing what you did. It takes incredible courage, and your perspective is so healthy. I just think it's really amazing, especially for a woman. You're incredibly brave." His words were like oxygen filling my empty lungs. I knew in my heart it was the brave choice, but to hear it on someone else's lips made all the difference.

Chapter 26

The Frequent Flyer

"Everything you have ever wanted,
is sitting on the other side of fear."
—George Addair

THE MINUTE I engaged a divorce lawyer, I signed up for a trip to
Ecuador in the spring with other members of my church. Once I
decided to find my way out of my box, I thought a good place to
start would be as close to God as I could get. Our congregation had a
relationship with an orphanage in Quito called For His Children, and
groups of volunteers had visited since it was established by a couple
from California. I had wanted to go since I had first heard about it
years before but didn't think I was capable. Now, I didn't think; I just
signed the waiver and the deposit check. I was going.

We didn't travel much in the five years we were married. The
anticipatory anxiety surrounding our honeymoon flight to Greece

was a dark cloud that hung over our entire wedding. Then the terrorist attacks occurred on September 11, just two days after our arrival in Athens, and every flight after that became even more terrifying than I originally imagined. It added a whole new level of my fear of flying and set the tone for potential trips to come. Every time we discussed it, I lobbied convincingly to redirect our vacation money to new furniture needed to fill empty rooms in our house. He always agreed.

I can't say I regretted it. I loved feeling safe at home in my newly furnished living room, sitting by the fire and reading. Before I decided to leave my box, I did everything I could to make it as comfortable as possible.

And I didn't feel like I was missing out. For years, I let my fear of flying dictate how far from home I would venture. I let fear ground me, essentially. I looked at photos on the Internet and thought, "They are so beautiful; it's as if I'm there." I thought I could go anywhere in the world with a simple Google search. *Why feel the discomfort and take the risk when it's all right here at my fingertips?*

I justified my fear by convincing myself that pictures could replace experiences—that appreciation could replace real adventure. I hadn't yet experienced the critical mindset shift when a picture becomes an *invitation*, not an *alternative*. I hadn't yet realized that *the experience is what reminds us we are alive.*

I also convinced myself I hated to fly. I identified with my anxiety so much that it was hard to tell the difference between what I wanted and what the little girl was dictating. I could hardly discern between her voice and my own.

The night before, I'd lie awake filled with terror, imagining all that could go wrong—mechanical failures, terrorists, surface-to-air missiles, or just having to endure six hours of extreme turbulence. I'd wonder how the pilots were preparing. Were they out late partying? Will they be hungover or upset over a fight with their girlfriend, who also happens to be our flight attendant (which actually happened once)?

On my drive to the airport, I'd look back at my house in the rearview mirror, convinced I'd never see it again. When I boarded the plane, I'd peek into the cockpit and scan the area for alcohol or drug paraphernalia. I'd breathe in through my nose to detect any hint of marijuana or booze. I'd try to make eye contact with the pilots to confirm their pupils were dilating. I wished I could review their medical history, relationship status, and latest Facebook posts.

But secretly, I *loved* to fly. It reminded me of being free and wild, willing to ignore my comfort zone and explore my boundaries. It reminded me not of who I used to be, because I couldn't remember a time before anxiety, but of who I'd always been *underneath* the anxiety. My true self that was always there whispering to me and waiting for moments like this when I could actually hear it.

Flying was (and still is) one of the most exhilarating experiences in my life. I always chose the window seat and, for most of the flight, stared out at the landscape unfolding below me. I am in awe of the invention of the airplane and the riches it bestows on us. The ability to be transported anywhere on the globe in a matter of hours is astonishing, and just being up there is an adventure in and of itself.

I am grateful for the opportunity to fly like the birds, dance alongside the clouds, and have access to any place on this earth. To know my reach, my dreams, and my adventures were limited only by my fear, not by accessibility.

In finding my way out of the box, flying became my laboratory of exposure therapy. I had no choice but to listen to the stories I was telling myself and start to distinguish between the voice of the terrified little girl and the voice coming from someplace deeper inside me. I was forced to sit with the feelings each created and make choices based on how I wanted to show up for myself—and, ultimately, who I wanted to be.

On my way to Ecuador, shortly after we leveled off at our cruising altitude, a flight attendant made an announcement asking for any medical staff on board.

Of course! My first flight alone to challenge my boundaries, and the pilot is dying. I knew it! I screamed silently. After the second call for medical assistance, I jumped up and asked the flight attendant if the pilots were OK.

"If the pilots need medical attention, dear, we handle that privately, not over the intercom," she responded, which both calmed and terrified me. I offered her my Klonopin in case they needed to calm the passenger and took my seat.

The next time I saw a flight attendant, I asked about the passenger's status. She told me she was having a panic attack. *Panic! You don't need medical staff for panic*, I thought. *I just had three panic attacks waiting for your update, and you don't see me calling for medical staff.*

I thought about going back to sit with her and how I could comfort her. I imagined the conversation we would have.

"How are you feeling? I've had anxiety and panic attacks for as long as I can remember, and I know exactly how you're feeling. I've been exactly where you are."

I hug her. Actually, I hold her, long and tight, to absorb her fear and panic and digest it for her.

I look deep into her eyes and ask, "What are you most afraid of?" Then I ask her if that fear is real or just a story. She confirms it's just a story. I smile and confidently nod my head, whispering, "We land. I know we do."

I continue, "There are only two options. We fly and crash, or we fly and land. But in this moment, we can't control either outcome;

we can only control our own state of being, our own thoughts, until one or the other happens. Based on either outcome, we should enjoy every second of this flight. That's all we've got. We already made the courageous choice to get on the plane. Now we ride that courage out until this flight ends. Until then, I'm here for you. Tell me everything. You can be vulnerable and scared. You are safe with me."

I took a deep breath and opened my eyes. I felt a deep connection to this woman, and I didn't even know her. Something softened inside of me, and in a moment, I realized that hug, that speech, that comfort and compassion—it was all for me. That person in the back of the plane panicking was my little girl. Her voice was becoming very clear, and so was mine.

Chapter 27

The Traveler

*"If you do not push the boundaries,
you will never know where they are."*
—T.S. Elliot

WHEN I STARTED this journey out of my box, I knew there was no map to guide me. I would have to set out and find my own way. I had to test the strength of those walls, push the boundaries, and test my limits. I had to push aside the debris to uncover the lines I'd drawn in the sand, so I could build my capacity and courage to see and step beyond them. I had to expose myself to situations where I would be forced to face my fears and choose to live the life I dreamed of and be the woman I knew that I was despite the anxiety.

My fear of dying was surmounted only by my fear of not fully living, and traveling out of my comfort zone, literally and figuratively, made me feel alive again. I did what I thought would kill me, and I survived.

Ecuador

"Sit down. No, it's fine, sweetie. Go ahead and sit. Kristin, take Javier, please. Napkins! We need more napkins!" I tried to keep the other children calm as Estrella lost control. I felt the people around us staring and heard muffled comments in Spanish, which I could hardly make out.

Given I had met Estrella only three days prior, I knew she was prone to outbursts, but I had no idea what could set her off. This time, it was our lunch in the middle of the food court of a local mall. Something agitated her, so drinks were tossed, hamburgers were thrown, and Estrella was now sitting under the table, banging her clenched fist on the floor.

It was ironic how much I could relate to her being fine one minute and under the table the next. I couldn't always predict what would trigger a panic attack and how quickly I'd lose control. I felt like people were staring at me, and I'd want to bang my fist in frustration with myself. It could be the chaos of the food court, the loud noises, or other children not listening to instruction. It all made perfect sense to me. Watching it from a safe distance gave me a new perspective. I could see myself so clearly in her. The understanding and compassion I felt for her were now seeping into my own bones.

I stayed under the table with her until she was ready to emerge unscathed… except for some ketchup on her shirt. As I cleaned up the mess and calmed the other children with my fellow chaperones, I noticed my hands shaking. There was so much emotion running through my body I would need to contain it before it grew into a panic attack. I tried to stop it, wondering who would calm me down if I ended up under that table. I couldn't even speak Spanish, and we were still far from the orphanage. Normally this would have made me feel trapped and escalated my panic. But I pictured crawling back under that table and envisioned myself going back under to save me. Just like I did with Estrella. And with that, I started to cry. I couldn't hold the emotions back anymore without hyperventilating. I had to let them out or be devoured by them. I excused myself, found a bathroom, locked myself in a stall, and bawled until I felt like a dishrag. Then I put my sunglasses on and returned to the group.

Taking this trip by myself was an enormous step outside my comfort zone. I needed vaccines that could cause hallucinations, the orphanage sat at 9,350 feet above sea level, and I had forgotten 99% of my Spanish. Quito was also a very dangerous city at the time. The orphanage was behind walls with access gates. Military guards with machine guns held post at the entrance of the grocery store. And the walk through the airport parking lot required a male escort for any woman daring to find her ride. But my church group provided just the support I needed to forge on regardless.

I brought my Klonopin, but it was more like a magic feather than a crutch. I liked the idea of having it with me, but I tried not to take it, fearing a bad reaction would land me in the medical care of a third-world country. I had little access to other buffers like food and alcohol living in a common house and sleeping in bunk beds with my fellow church volunteers. So, I wrote in my journal each night and prayed a lot.

My fight or flight response was slightly triggered all day given the safety issues and unpredictable nature of taking care of infants and older children with disabilities, so I was actually in a strange comfort zone. The anxiety came in the quiet moments when I felt like I needed to get out of there and go home. I could feel the panic mount but started hearing it as almost outside of me. I knew so deeply that I was exactly where I wanted to be and where I belonged in that moment. It was stretching and teaching me, and I could see that so clearly. The anxious and intrusive thoughts felt old and stale, yet I gave them compassion thinking about Estrella under the table. Ultimately, I didn't experience a single panic attack.

Being there was a blessing to both the giver and the receiver and made me feel close to the sacred. I knew I was witnessing God's work, and I longed to be a part of it. The most profound gift I received was the divine perspective of witnessing pure, unconditional love. Despite being born perfectly healthy, some children were abandoned by their parents at the hospital the minute they were born. Some were taken from abusive and unstable homes, and others were left for dead in parks with disabilities so severe they would be orphaned forever. And at this orphanage, they were all loved despite having parents who were broken, despite having their own disabilities, and despite being abandoned by those who should have loved them first. They were loved without having had done anything—without performing or being perfect. They were loved simply because they were born, and someone thought that was enough.

Sedona

Upon arriving home and feeling energized by living through my travel to Ecuador, I booked a trip to Arizona in June. I would drive from the Phoenix airport to a spa in Sedona for one night and then drive on to Las Vegas, where my brother was living. This time, I was going it alone—the flight, the drive—no church group to offer some sense of safety and security. Just a flip phone and a folded map.

When I told my soon-to-be-ex-husband about my travel plans, he told me he was traveling to Phoenix to see his sister on the same day. I thought it was fate. I thought that if he heard of my trip to

Ecuador and my courage in coming to Arizona alone, he would see that my anxiety didn't control me anymore and that maybe I was worth fighting for.

I asked if he wanted to meet for a drink in the airport, and he said, "Maybe. Let's see how the flights work out. Let's talk in Phoenix." While his response didn't thrill me, I thought it was hopeful. There was a part of me that thought I had already made such significant strides that I could actually go back to him and make it work.

The flight was terrifying, so I drank vodka. But not too much, ever, that I didn't remain vigilant and prepared to take over at any time should the pilots fail to be able to fulfill their duties in the cockpit. I arrived around 10 p.m. and immediately called him. I left a voice message and texted him. I grabbed my carry-on, checking my phone periodically. Nothing. I found my rental car and checked my phone again. Nothing. I called one last time. Nothing. I couldn't believe I'd come this far, and he was still unmoved and unimpressed.

I checked into my shady motel by the airport. And by shady, I don't mean it was surrounded by trees. It was close to midnight by then, and I hadn't eaten since I left Boston. When I called the front desk for room service, he laughed and hung up. Not surprised or terribly disappointed, I searched out a candy machine chained to the cement wall outside, ran back to my room with my Snickers, and fell asleep in my clothes on top of the stained bedspread.

I woke at the break of dawn and checked my phone. Nothing. I decided that was the last time. No more checking, wondering, or hoping. I was done and on my own now. I dropped the top of the convertible and started my drive to Sedona. I turned the radio up all the way and sang at the top of my lungs. On long straightaways, I took my hands off the wheel and threw them over my head, feeling the wind stream through my fingers. I wasn't looking at a picture of the beauty of Arizona. I was there! I wasn't living in a Google search, I was in my own adventure. I wasn't appreciating two-dimensional beauty from a safe distance; I was a part of it. I was living my life, and I could feel it in every inch of my body as the red rocks unfolded in front of me.

Upon arrival, I drove straight to my scheduled Pink Jeep tour. The thought of it terrified me, so I knew I had to do it. I got there early, Klonopin stashed in my pockets, and found my driver early to explain my anxiety situation. He seemed sympathetic and saved me the front seat. He did not, however, water down the tour because of it.

In case you've never taken one, these tours travel into the red rocks and drive as if defying gravity. I thought we would tip over several times. But even while I heard the worst-case scenarios swirling in my mind and felt my heart racing, I loved every minute of it. The excitement and thrill of it reminded me that I was never afraid of living my life. Like flying or skiing. I actually wanted to do all of it. *That* is what tore me apart. She wouldn't let me. She caged me in that box unwillingly and convinced me that if these adventures didn't kill me, the anxiety would.

This was a tipping point. I was ready to risk the anxiety, to call her bluff and see if it was worth it. I was coming out of the shadows, and there was no going back. And my new perspective meant I expected the panic, so I didn't push it away. I took it along for the adventure and rode it out when it hit me. I knew it was coming, and I did it anyway because I had to see what my life could be like on the outside of that box.

When we stopped halfway through the ride to get out and marvel at the views, I walked out to a spot far from the Jeep and the others on my tour. I sat with my back to them and inhaled deeply. The view was majestic, like nothing I'd ever seen. I wasn't sure how I had gotten there, but I didn't want to leave. I didn't feel that tightness in my chest or have the intense need to run away. I felt the sacredness of the space, and my body tingled with an unforgettable life force I couldn't deny. It was as if my anxious energy had changed color or frequency. It wasn't pushing me under, but rather lifting me out. I was finding myself again. My sacred self.

The next morning, I woke just before dawn to attend a yoga class at the spa across a creek from my bungalow. I had only done yoga about four times in my life at that point, but if I was going to try number five, this was the place. A layer of fog blanketed the earth, rising only about four feet off the ground, and created a dream-like walk through an enchanted forest.

As I crossed a footbridge, I was startled at the sound of something moving by the creek. I stopped walking and saw a deer drinking at the water's edge. As I watched her move through the fog, my eyes adjusted and discovered another deer just beside her, and then another and another, until it seemed hundreds had appeared for as far as my eye could see. It took my breath away, and I found myself unable to move.

At that moment, I felt the Universe expanding before me, revealing its magic and wonder—that is, if I would be brave enough to step out and meet it.

Italy

Upon arriving home again, I booked another trip. It wouldn't be until the next fall because I needed to finalize the divorce and save some money, but I already felt like a different person and wanted to keep my momentum. The anxiety wasn't gone by any stretch of my imagination, but I had found just enough oxygen to continue moving around my box—discovering my limits and testing them.

I would take a guided group bus tour through Italy in October. A foreign country with no one I knew, a language I didn't speak, strangers I couldn't escape, and a bus I couldn't get off of. It was a perfect cocktail of anxiety triggers.

I went from being surrounded by beloved church members and orphans to being completely alone in the desert, to being confined to a tour bus with total strangers for 10 days. My social anxiety was hidden well but very real. Sometimes those who struggle with anxiety and depression are perceived as outgoing and social. That is usually a defense mechanism to hide what is really going on below the surface. So, while I was extremely uncomfortable, I knew without challenge there would be no change. I also knew there was no threat to my safety and security, so I would need to take care of that scared little girl inside of me if I was going to take this adventure.

The first night in Rome, still high from the adrenaline of flying to Italy alone, finding my group, and settling into the hotel, I snuck out. I didn't want to start my trip with 20 other people being told where to go and when. Not yet. I needed to get out and explore on my own first. I needed to prove to myself that this was all really happening.

I walked the streets surrounding the Coliseum in awe. As the light faded, I came to a fountain lit from beneath the water. It lit me up as well. I wanted more of everything I was feeling, so I walked and walked for hours until I found the St. Regis Hotel. I marveled at the enormous door, then opened it to find the most majestic lobby I'd ever seen. And it was completely empty. It was all mine. I felt like Beauty stepping into Beast's castle—but *after* they fall in love. I walked into the sprawling bar and ordered champagne and one of everything on the dessert menu. This is what it felt like to be out of my box. This is the life I couldn't live looking at pictures on the Internet. I sat and ate and let Rome seep into my bones.

As we traveled south, I continued reading the book I started on the flight over, *A Thousand Days in Venice*. In the book, an American woman finds love while on vacation in Venice and doesn't return home until the relationship ends years later. The images unfolded on those pages and tantalized me as we continued on our tour with Venice only days away.

My mind felt safe within the structure of the daily schedule of driving, eating, and touring with the group, which allowed me to explore my surroundings—and, in turn, my walls—when I had alone time. I explored on my own and felt resistance at every turn. I heard the little girl warning me and telling me to wait in my hotel room until it was time to leave. Again, it all felt familiar but tiring. Resisting the flow exhausted me for years, and it was time to let go. It was like holding back an inevitable tide, and I couldn't do it anymore. And the fact that no one here knew me, which in the past would have caused more anxiety, now gave me permission to try on being someone new, being the person I was searching for beyond those walls.

My favorite night was sitting in the square on Capri. The blue and gold buildings were lit up by strings of lights. I sat outside at a tavern with all the patrons under a blanket of stars. I was on an island on the other side of the world. I didn't speak the language or even know if there were medical facilities. I should have felt terrified, but I'd never felt so safe and at peace. I felt the Universe lifting my head above water to breathe and giving me a boost to peek over the walls to see and feel what was on the other side. Then all I wanted was more.

Once in Venice, my group visited the Gallerie dell'Accademia and Doge's Palace first. The stories and their heroes pulled me in, and I fell in love with how they made me feel—brave, beautiful, and timeless.

Once on my own, I stared at the map of the city that reminded me of a house of mirrors. My guide's warnings confirmed my fears that the map was not accurate and navigating your way is nearly impossible to anyone but the locals. I felt the anxiety stirring inside, but I knew I had to go. I heard the voice negotiating and justifying, and then I whispered to it, "*You can be afraid, but we're going.*" If I was going to die of anxiety, Venice was certainly the place to do it!

I walked the streets alone and got deliciously lost, just as predicted. I ate my way through tiny alleys that weren't even marked on my map. I was afraid and excited, and it made me feel the same physically as when I felt anxious—vibrations, pit in my stomach, increased heart rate—but this time, I felt alive.

When I finally found my way out, I sat on the steps in St. Mark's Square with a glass of prosecco, watching couples kiss, pigeons play, and curtains blow in the breeze. Unlike the character in my book who fell in love with a person, I took in every detail and fell in love with a city.

Rainbows

Don't offer me your rainbows. Their brilliant colors hurt my eyes.

If I could reach, I'd strip them one by one to organize my thoughts.

And as for their promises of pots of gold, I'm not comfortable with coins. And I would never travel that far to find them.

So much for your fight against the dying of the light.

I had no choice whether it was wrong or right.

Instead, promise you'll sit with me for one more sunset,

sharing shades of brilliance we felt but never spoke of and will never forget.

Hold me as the golden light fades and darkness overtakes us.

Wait with me while the stars are lit slowly, one by one, until a sparkling canvas covers our sky, setting off a symphony of nocturnes and dancing fires.

And we'll watch them dazzle—all the wonders of love and life.

Chapter 28

The Therapists

"When I let go of what I am,
I become what I might be."
—Lao Tzu

On my flight home from Italy, I wondered where I would go next on my journey. I didn't have enough money to just keep traveling, but I was committed to my progress, so I decided my next trip would be back to therapy. I wanted to find and push some boundaries internally now.

The first time I tried therapy was in college, when my anxious and depressive thoughts turned suicidal. It was a Monday when I called the counseling center on campus to make an appointment. Their first available was Thursday afternoon. I confirmed, then wondered how I would survive all of the minutes until then.

"So, what brings you here today?" he asked.

I shook my head, terrified to speak the words. I was convinced that saying them out loud would unleash their power over me.

"Are you feeling overwhelmed by school? Did you have an unwanted sexual encounter? Do you feel depressed or anxious? Do you feel homesick?" he looked up from his pad of paper as if he'd been reading from a list.

I didn't know where to start or who to be. I felt numb, yet, at the same time, so uncomfortable I wanted to jump out of my own skin. *This guy will have me committed if I tell him what is running through my mind on a daily basis*, I thought.

I looked out the window expressionless, his voice trailing off into the distance as he continued to cajole a response.

After another awkward 10 minutes vacillating between silence and his solitary banter, I finally spoke, "You know what? I totally forgot I have this assignment I need to turn in. I'm really sorry, but I have to go." I grabbed my bag and left without looking back. I never returned.

I tried another therapist the following semester when I returned home, hoping to find myself again, rather than travel abroad to Mexico. She asked me what I was feeling and why I decided to come in for a visit. My responses were given by a person desperate to keep the real answers to those questions locked away in the deep recesses of her mind.

My safe place was not defined by the person sitting across from me. It was no easier for me to reveal my thoughts and feelings to a therapist than a family member or friend. At the time, it was defined by how deep I had pushed my scary thoughts into the shadows. My comfort level and ability to function were measured by the distance between my current thoughts and the thoughts I'd locked away. If I acknowledged their existence to a therapist, they would come rushing out, filling my head and veins with pure panic—like freebasing anxiety.

While the therapist would have the satisfaction of understanding "what I was feeling and why I came in," I would be left alone in my anxious frenzy and depressive fog until I could push them back into the shadows and lock them away. So, I chose to keep my distance and my conversation surface level, which did nothing to help my condition.

In my late-20s, I tried therapy again after that drive home from Boston, convinced I was losing my mind. I was also struggling with eating disorders and my relationship with Jack at the time and needed someone to help me better understand why irrational fears were taking over my life.

Jane was the first therapist I met with, and I hired her on the spot. I had no capacity to hold "tryouts" for the best fit, given my condition. She was also the first to prescribe me Klonopin.

Our conversations were similar to all the others: surface-level anxiety and weight issues. Self-love and positive body image weren't something people talked about at the time. The medication didn't give me the courage to explore my terrifying and unmanageable thoughts, so we agreed I could solve most of my issues by breaking up with Jack and staying under a certain weight. I did both and became more anxious than ever. I took a refill of the prescription and only went back to her when I needed more.

When I hit rock bottom and was completely unable to talk to a therapist, I would listen to hours and hours of recordings of group therapy sessions from the Midwest Center for Anxiety and Depression. In this, I found a new awareness of what was happening when I had a thought and how that thought created a physical reaction. I learned about the torturous "what if" cycle and gained a "bag of tools" I could use to avoid, recognize, and deal with my next panic attack. It was the best therapy I'd gotten so far. It allowed me to get back on my feet, leave the house, go to work, and get my life back, confident I wasn't alone, I wasn't crazy, and I could manage or avoid my next attack.

But they were coping skills, not a silver bullet ridding me of anxiety forever. While life-saving at the time, I was still in my box, clutching a Klonopin in one hand and a Starbucks coffee in the other.

These new tools were a double-edged sword. They helped me function again, but they also taught me how to accommodate my anxiety and masterfully hide my struggles from others—and sometimes, even myself. I was becoming much more productive, so much so that there were times I was consumed in the living rather than the healing, so the anxiety always found its way back in.

When I announced my divorce, I found Karen. She was a lovely and supportive psychologist. She affirmed my decisions and boosted my self-confidence, so I chose to spend time with her. She helped me navigate my way through the dark tunnel of guilt and shame, the inevitable by-products of leaving my husband. But when it came to discussing my anxiety and panic, we only skimmed the surface. Again, the protocol was, "If we fix the things that logically cause people anxiety, then it will just go away." Again, it decidedly did not.

I still feared a deeper dive would expose more than I could handle, so I couldn't identify the root of my pain and source of my anxiety. I was only starting my journey, and without a map, I was lost. As a result, my sessions became more like chatting with a girlfriend over coffee. Once I sold the house and moved, I tried to keep a consistent schedule because I genuinely loved spending time with Karen, but the drives became burdensome, so I left to try living life on my own.

I decided to give it one last shot on my flight home from Italy. I was making so much progress I felt confident I could discuss anything, dive as deep as they wanted, and get to the root of my disorders.

I found Kate through a mutual friend. She asked probing questions, and I gave more honest answers than I had ever in the past. I put my cards on the table and let them fall where they may. I'd follow her advice and do the work. I was ready.

It felt scary and amazing and life-giving, as if a boulder had been removed from my back. Sitting on her couch completely vulnerable, I waited optimistically as she took notes. While I was prepared for the work, I wasn't prepared for her response.

Here we go again, I thought. Someone telling me I *am* my thoughts, my emotions, my rationalizations. I am a prisoner of my current condition. In our very first meeting, she all but confirmed that "leaving my box" wasn't really an option for me. She said my family history and the environment in which I was raised had planted seeds that were now rooted deep inside of me and could not be eradicated. While I shouldn't have been surprised, I was hoping for a more open mind.

My biggest disappointment was the labeling. I believe labeling can be very powerful, and thus should be done with caution. When we label with positive affirmations, it allows us to fully embody that positivity rather than just experience it. For instance, you can experience kindness or compassion by extending or receiving it, or you can embody them by being kind and compassionate. They are not just things you are doing, but they become who you are.

Alternatively, when we label with negative affirmations, it requires us to embody the negativity rather than experience it from a safe distance. If you are having panic attacks or depressive thoughts, you don't want to be labeled as disordered or clinically depressed. Then these are no longer circumstances—they become who you are. It sounds much different than, "You are currently experiencing anxiety or feeling depressed." These statements describe circumstances, not personal characteristics. Circumstances leave space for hope—you can change them or change the way you think about them, both of which give you back control and change your path.

I struggled with her assessment and with her confirmation that my box was exactly where I should be. She even applauded my management skills.

"You have disorders, and they should be accommodated and medicated accordingly so you can live as fully as possible with them," she said.

"Well, what if I don't want to live with them?" I asked.

"That's likely not an option for you as I see it," she replied dryly, as if my life wasn't hanging in the balance.

"Well, that's too bad," I said. "I guess I'll have to find my way without you. Thanks for your time." I stood up, grabbed my coat, and left her office.

In my 20s and early 30s, I would have agreed with her. But once that whisper deep inside me became a roar, they didn't even discourage me. I felt strangely empowered by it. Like I was headed back into the garage before anyone else was awake to earn that trophy whether I had the skill or not. I may have disorders, but I also have heart and determination. And if anyone can do it, it'll be me.

She gifted me that tenacity, and this—I no longer thought I needed the right therapist to find my way. She sealed the deal. I was on my own and completely comfortable with that.

I don't want to sound like I'm against therapy or finding a psychiatrist, psychologist, counselor, or whatever works for your specific condition. It has helped millions of people with a variety of issues, and I completely support it.

I simply struggled to find the right person—and *be* the right person. I felt like a square peg sitting on the couch staring into a round abyss. I wasn't able to reveal myself in ways I should have. And I didn't have the capacity to find the right person for my particular needs. As a result, I never found the relief or the healing I sought. But the Universe had other plans and kept pushing me in another direction.

Chapter 29

The Bags

*"The cave you fear to enter holds the
treasure you seek."*
—Joseph Campbell

THE QUESTIONS BEFORE ME remained ...

Could I ever drop the bags full of anxiety and my tools to cope? They were so heavy that I could barely lift them anymore.

Could I ever free myself from anxiety? Could I live without constantly accommodating and letting it chip away at my freedom? Could I move beyond the walls of my box to live my fullest life?

I had tested my boundaries and seen glimpses of what life could look like—holding orphans in Ecuador, driving through the Arizona desert, and throwing coins in the Trevi Fountain. I was on my own now and ready to find those answers.

So, I went on a quest. How does one begin a quest, you ask? Well, I Googled it. Yup. I Googled "quest" because I couldn't get the word out of my head and wanted to read the definition. And in Googling it, I found an online course through The Chopra Center literally called "The Quest." The Universe isn't always subtle. What could be more perfect?

I hoped this course would provide some answers, or at least point me in the right direction. Deepak Chopra and Martha Beck gave lectures and held live, interactive calls. During one such call, Martha chose the question I submitted so I could be coached one on one.

I asked, "If I have been struggling with anxiety my entire life, could I ever overcome that burden and start living anxiety-free? Could I stop preparing for the next panic attack? Is preparing prudent or preventive? Can I leave my condition and my mental constructs inside the box and step outside without my bag of tools? If not, is it possible to carry this burden and live my fullest life? If walking away from it is possible, what is the first step? What if I take that first step and immediately have a panic attack? Does it mean I stepped in the wrong direction or the right one?

I realized that was a lot for one call, but I needed to speak the words out loud, and once I started, I couldn't stop. Just like speaking my scary thoughts made them tangible and terrifying, speaking my truth now made the beginning of my quest feel just as real.

Martha talked about using fear as fuel and embracing the panic, physical symptoms, and anxious thoughts rather than pushing them further into the shadows. This sounded interesting.

First, I thought, *If I could use my fear as fuel, I could power a mission to Mars.* It takes commitment and stamina to be an anxious person. I was constantly analyzing and assessing, strategizing, and obsessing over every detail of my inner and outer world to keep the anxiety in check. What if I could harness all of that energy and use those skills to find my way out of this box?

Second, my shadows were at maximum capacity. I had pushed so much in there I couldn't even fit a pack of dental floss at this point. So, what if I used this fuel and commitment and stamina to walk in there and face what I'd been running from for so long? What if, by going into the shadows, I could find out what had caused my anxiety in the first place and heal it rather than hiding from it?

That was when my journey started to take form. Fearing my anxious thoughts and fighting against them was only making them stronger. I would have to go into the cave I feared most to find my answers. But where was the cave? Was there more than one?

It was just a few weeks later that I had the life-changing vision in my meditation when I found myself staring face-to-face with that angry Wizard of Oz. Upon seeing that little girl behind the curtain pulling the levers, I suddenly realized that the first cave I had to go into was that cardboard box. I couldn't reject that part of myself and abandon her. She represented all of my anxiety, and I needed to bring her out of the shadows—out of that box. Then I needed to take her on this journey with me, to face the fears and understand the pain that perpetuated the panic. I had been looking outside myself for the answer for decades, with little relief. Now it was time to go *within* to find my way out.

Chapter 30

Soul Food

"If you trade your authenticity for safety,
you may experience the following: anxiety,
depression, eating disorders, addiction, rage,
blame, resentment, and inexplicable grief."
—Brené Brown

GULP. I WISH I'd had that quote in my 20s.

I believe healthy living is paramount to overcoming anxiety. Physical homeostasis has been key to my mental well-being, and it took me a long time to get to that place.

I no longer think about what to eat every second of the day or struggle with my weight in an endless loop of negative self-talk and destructive behaviors. I don't use food to punish myself or buffer against my emotional angst. I don't panic when I gain a few pounds or when I reach my goal weight. That may sound strange, but when I saw those numbers on the scale that I'd been dreaming of for months, I was so desperate to hold on to it that I became paralyzed with fear. Now, I am at peace with both gain and loss, knowing they are fleeting and temporary, and I am able to rebalance at any time because food no longer has the power over me it once did. When I took back that power, I took back control over my body and mind.

I didn't come to terms with my struggle until I witnessed my mother's struggle with her weight finally end when she developed chemotherapy-induced anorexia. She was diagnosed with pancreatic cancer and began treatment at 180 pounds. She lost sixty pounds in two months.

I tried to make light of it when I realized she would surely die. Laughter is a priceless commodity when that truth sinks in.

"Finally!" I shouted. "How long have we been waiting to see that number?" She laughed lightly, like it hurt a little. I cringed inside and held back the tears.

When her clothes started falling off, we shopped together for a whole new wardrobe. As we rifled through the racks, it felt very different than when we used to triumphantly do the same thing after our Weight Watchers meetings. Now she had no choice, and the new clothes brought no joy. We smiled awkwardly and made jokes about Workout World and tuna salads to lighten the mood, both knowing it was the size she would be buried in.

I didn't want to wait for something tragic to happen to me in order to find peace with my body, always wanting to look and feel different and blaming myself when I couldn't make it happen. Seeing her lying there in a hospital bed, wasting away under the knit cap they gave her to keep her warm, I realized the numbers were all an illusion.

This was part of my journey. I needed to heal the pain to release the perfectionism and end the punishment. The anxiety it caused was immeasurable, and I couldn't do it anymore. I couldn't waste so much time and brainpower every single day judging myself for the number on the scale, journaling everything that went into my mouth, counting calories in and out, bracing myself for restaurants and vacations. Eventually, the battle ends—not because you finally won, but because you realize there was never any war to begin with.

As I shifted my focus to my mental health, becoming more self-aware, I began managing my weight with self-love rather than self-loathing. I stopped using food to hide from my feelings. When I was temporarily soothed by that crutch, it kept me from forming the deep connection with myself that comes from actually sitting with the anxiety rather than avoiding it.

So that's what I did. I sat with the anxiety without any lifelines—no phone calls, no medication, and no food. I explored the discomfort in each part of my body—the shortness of breath, the shaking hands, the erratic heartbeat. I allowed the emotions to spread into every inch of my body.

I listened intently with a compassionate ear as my thoughts catastrophized, intent on convincing me that death was imminent. "Run. Run!" I heard them repeat over and over. But instead, I sat. *Run where?* I thought. *There is no place safer than right here.* So, I waited to see what came next, assuring myself that it was not death, and I was safe.

And just when I thought I was tearing open at the seams, everything inside me quieted. I felt only a subtle vibration. My breath was deep and steady, and my mind was calm. The part of me that I had caged in that box was being reborn. In the fire's blaze, I didn't burn. I came alive. In the same way that food turned from a savior to an oppressor, sitting in the fire I thought would destroy me actually brought me back to life.

Chapter 31

The Reluctant Yogi

*"It does not matter how slowly you go,
as long as you don't stop."*
—Confucius

MAYBE YOU ARE LIKE ME and had always practiced a regular, rigorous exercise program but stopped exercising altogether because of anxiety. Scientists have found that just five minutes of aerobic exercise can begin to stimulate anti-anxiety effects. Psychologists studying the subject suggest that a 10-minute walk may be just as good as a 45-minute workout.[19]

Studies also show that the best exercises for reducing the symptoms of anxiety are biking, hiking, running, brisk walking, yoga, and tennis. I've tried them all. Here are my experiences with three of those as I found my way back from the brink.

Running

In *Your Next Big Thing: 10 Small Steps to Get Moving and Get Happy*, Ben Michaelis, Ph.D., concludes that, "Running causes lasting changes in our 'feel good' neurotransmitters serotonin and norepinephrine, both during and after exercise. What's more: The repetitive motions of running appear to have a meditative effect on the brain."

To this I can attest! When I crossed the finish line, I had never been so proud of myself and, at the same time, so sure I would never run a full marathon. I had just finished my first, and my last, *half* marathon. While I had no desire to ever run that far again unless being chased, I will never forget or underestimate the significance of that accomplishment. My journey from the couch to that finish line came literally one step at a time.

When I first met Greg, he had just run the New York City Marathon. In contrast, my exercise routine had devolved into walking through the grocery store, holding onto a shopping cart to keep me steady. But in my glow of new love and something to distract and possibly even save me from my anxious state, I agreed to join him on his short run days.

But first, as always, I presented my list of requirements. I would run only a mile from the house, no further. That way, if something bad happened, I could walk back home in under 30 minutes. He had to stop and wait each time I checked my heart rate, which was about every five minutes. In his glow of new love, he agreed. At the time, he innocently saw me as a "non-runner" and a willing participant. He didn't realize he was looking at the tip of an iceberg. So, he had a running buddy, and I had a new lifeline.

When we were still living in different states, on my walks alone I was motivated to venture a little further from the house each day and then jog back, adding a little more space between me and the safety of my apartment each time. I even started exploring to the far corners of the grocery store without a cart. Not to buy anything, of course, just to see if I could make it all the way back to the registers without incident.

At first, I would look at each telephone pole and say, "I'll run to that pole, and if I need to stop, I will." Eventually, I'd reach the pole and ask, do I stop, or do I challenge myself? I started with 10 poles, then 20, and further and further until I stopped counting. However, there were also many failed attempts.

As I passed each house, I analyzed whether it seemed like a safe place to approach if I needed a bathroom, or water, or had to call 911. Still, I never ran that far from home. As my stamina increased, I started doing "victory laps." If I ran a few miles and made it safely back, I would run around my own block as many times as I could, knowing I was close to safety. I was tethered, but at least I was running.

My running sustained me for about three years while I was still unable to enter a gym without a debilitating panic attack. When Greg moved out, it became more than just a return to physical activity as I desperately needed to metabolize the pain and fear and push the edges of my comfort zone. The day after he left, I started running longer and further away from home than ever before. It became a metaphor for leaving it all behind.

About a year later, while still waiting to finalize the divorce, I signed up for a half marathon. That fall, I ran it in under two hours. I can't overstate the physical and mental benefits I got from running through that intensely emotional time. My anxiety was omnipresent but manageable as I started to expose my walls and challenge my limitations.

Biking

The dream was to be riding in a flock of indoor bikers, in front of me, behind me, and on either side. It's dark with only the glow of a small light on the instructor's side table and the light that shines through the window in the door behind me. I am not monitoring anything, not my distance from the door, not my heart rate, not the minutes left in class. I'm completely immersed in the hill we are climbing.

I push my heels to the floor on each beat of the music, feeling the pressure building in my thighs as the resistance increases and the hill steepens, and in my mind's eye, I see my goal: a majestic hilltop with the sun shining behind it. I can almost feel the warmth and wind on my face.

The reality was much different. When I finally found my way back into the gym, I could only go at odd hours when I knew it would be empty. Over time, I was going regularly, knowing anxiety would rise up, and I would have to manage it as best I could. Occasionally, I abandoned my workout entirely to ride out my panic attack in the parking lot.

As I sought ways to test my limits, I identified spinning classes as one of my biggest fears. I had been terrified of them since the first time I saw a class: the dark room, the loud music, the crowd, and lack of exits. It hit every anxiety trigger point. Even on good days, I thought, "I will never do that. Ever!" Then once I tried it, I said, "I will never do that *again*. Ever!"

The first time was measured. I arrived early to get the bike closest to the door. I prepared myself for the mental discomfort more than the physical. I gave myself the option to just sit and pedal slowly if necessary. The goal was to simply stay on the bike until the end of class, regardless of what my feet were doing.

Once they turned off the lights, shut the door, and turned on the music, my heart raced, and I wasn't even pedaling yet. The music was so loud I wanted to jump out of my skin. The instructor screamed over it so we could hear her directives. It felt chaotic. I searched the room to assess the faces of other bikers, and they all appeared to be enjoying it. I could only think about how long I could last and when an appropriate time to exit would present itself. I continued to check my heart rate, and when I couldn't bring it below 165 bpm while barely pedaling, I grabbed my things and snuck out. Failure!

It took me years to go back, and I only agreed to go with a friend because I was convinced it couldn't have been as bad as I remembered. This time, I would have support, all the while thinking, "If she can do it …"

Throughout my first year of attending classes, if I could not secure a bike in the back near the door, I left before class even started. If I forgot my towel, my water, my watch to check my heart rate, or my noise-canceling headphones to drown out the deafening music and screaming instructor, I left.

What I didn't realize at the time was that not only was I abandoning class, I was abandoning myself. The lifelines I needed to merely start a class were adding up and turning into excuses to not challenge myself. Even with them, I still left class or just stopped pedaling because I couldn't catch my breath.

But by continuing to go back, despite what I considered failures, I discovered that over time, for as many times as I left, I stayed. Even when I didn't have a lifeline, if I stayed and survived, I felt something inside me shift. Every time I challenged myself to sit in the mental and physical discomfort and stay just a little longer, I felt an expansion and knew I was changing.

I remember the day I picked a bike in the front row, furthest from the door. There was no easy exit. In my mind, there would be eyes on my every move—every inhale, every gear change. I felt trapped and completely exposed before class even started.

Can I actually do this? I thought, gasping for air and watching others clip in effortlessly. About 20 minutes into the ride, as we crested the first hill, the instructor said, "Without challenge, there is no change. Let's go!"

And with that, I drove my heels down, inhaled deeply, and absorbed the moment into my bones. *If I can do this, what else am I capable of?*

It's in those moments that I fueled my positive feedback loop. I chipped away at the walls, and I sat in the light that shone through the cracks—feeling what awaited me on the other side.

I have since bought a Peloton and ride from home. Do I fear going back to group classes? Absolutely not. It's just far more accessible, convenient, and fun to pick my instructor, my music, and my ride. I ride just about every day, filling my tank with power and positivity as I grow stronger each time, both mentally and physically. Something that started as an impossibility became a long-term source of cardio fitness, joy, and empowerment.

Yoga

As someone who defines my memories by how well I was breathing at the time, finding my breath in yoga and linking it to movement has become an expression of self-love and care. Each class is an opportunity to find a sense of peace and calm amid my mental and physical discomfort. One of my instructor's gurus says, "If you're not breathing, you're dying." That rang true for me, literally, and I see it play out in yoga every day.

Classes became a training ground. The more I visited my discomfort and sat in it, the more it dissipated and allowed me the opportunity to find what lay beyond—true peace and power beyond measure.

I first tried yoga in my 20s when a therapist suggested it. She thought it would relax me. She thought wrong. My mind was sprinting in circles at the bottom of the well I was in, so if I wasn't crazy already, downward dog would surely get me there. The silence alone drove me mad. The idea of being alone with my thoughts for any amount of time was terrifying. When I tried it alone in my bedroom a few times, I never got past the first sun salutation. So, I quit yoga and found a new therapist.

I came back to the mat occasionally in my 30s, maybe once a year. My self-critic loved it! I would have at least one judgmental thought for each minute that I survived class. I set my mat down in the back near my escape route. Oftentimes, I did just that—escaped, only to feel ashamed and frustrated until a new source of shame took its place. It would take me about a year to forget how bad it was, then I would try again.

At the time, I was living in a place of resistance and isolation. I was actually afraid to stretch out because I knew there was pain locked away in my muscles and feared awakening it. I couldn't fathom the idea that my mind and body could work together to create balance and peace.

I thought that if I slowed down, the pain and fear would catch up to me, or if I opened myself up and let it in, it would destroy me. I thought my tension was my strength, holding the door shut as the anxiety ceaselessly pushed and pushed to pry it open. I was constant yang with no yin.

It wasn't until I was in my 40s and my mother was diagnosed with cancer that I came back to the mat and decided to stay, whatever the results. I was spinning regularly and realized quickly that you can't start crying in the middle of a challenging hill without hyperventilating. But I could cry on my mat. So, that's what I did. I came to my mat every day with every emotion—the anxiety, the fear, the pain, the grief—to see what I would find, both mentally and physically.

It wasn't easy. I started in the back again and gave myself permission to stop at any time and just relax in child's pose. But I couldn't leave the mat, because that would be abandoning myself. I needed to stay with all that was coming to the surface and making me so uncomfortable I wanted to flee. That was the work.

My yoga instructors would often say, "Root down and rise." At first, I took it literally. I grounded my feet into my mat and lifted my arms to the sky. And it felt as if I was cracking myself open to a Universe that would accept my pain and offer its healing.

As that healing journey progressed, it spoke to me on a new level. It said, "When you fall into a hole, don't climb out immediately. Don't run before the magic happens. Stay for as long as you need. Gather nutrients, rest, prune the parts that are naturally dying away, and build the strength you need to grow out. If you climb out right away or press fast-forward out of fear, all you've gained are some bruises and scars. Stay and soften into your hard places. Dare to surrender and see what you become."

And that's what I did. I surrendered. I got dizzy, I hyperventilated, and I cried a lot. But over time, it gave me a place to grieve, to celebrate, to find my center, and completely let go. I found space in my body to release all that I was holding onto so desperately and for so long and a silent center in my mind to just be still. Physically, I found a new awareness and appreciation for my body. Mentally, I found a deep peace and an authentic voice that had been quieted for too long. And I found a connection between the two that created the foundation for all the work that would come after. Through the lens of anxiety, my body and mind were the enemy. Now, they were the source of power I needed on my journey inward to find my sacred balance.

Taking Flight

By moonlit lakes and sunlit streams
I lose myself and find my dreams
At least for a time, it seems.

With a crooked smile and sparkling eyes
I spread my wings and soar the skies
Most of all, to my own surprise.

Chapter 32

The Meditation

"My mind is like a bad neighborhood.
I try not to go there alone."
—Anne Lamont

CULTIVATING A MEDITATION practice was always something I thought
I *should* do but didn't think I *could* do. At times I was able to string
together several minutes at a time, but the lack of immediate relief
from my symptoms made me easily distracted by other "quick-fixes"
and disillusioned by the promises of peace and empowerment. I struggled to find the patience or the point. But eventually and unexpect-
edly, my practice blossomed into the source of transformation I was
searching for.

My first experience was with the relaxation meditation on the CDs
from the MCAD. The guide walked me through a jungle where I
envisioned every detail, heard the crunch of leaves and sticks under

my feet, felt the sun on my face, smelled the lush grasses and flowers, and listened to the birds sing. There were always birds. It was similar to the 5-4-3-2-1 technique I still use today to calm my fight-or-flight response.[20] With my imagination stimulating my senses, there was no room left for my racing thoughts.

The meditation ended at a waterfall that collected into a pool where I would sit on a rock and breathe. Sitting by that waterfall became my safe place, and I tried to go back there whenever I felt a panic attack coming.

I didn't consider this meditation at the time because I would never have sat alone with my own thoughts. But I found walking through a jungle of my own creation with a guide far less terrifying.

Over the years, my aversion to meditation remained and had several layers. First, I knew there were still terrifying thoughts buried deep in my mind that, when exposed, would ignite into an inferno of anxiety and depression. The better I felt mentally, the more I avoided going in there even with a licensed professional.

Second, I still believed my thoughts were me. I identified with them. I thought they were what made me who I was. When I read that the goal of meditation was to sit in the space between your thoughts, I was convinced I would vanish. The idea of having no thoughts terrified me. Where was I if there were no thoughts? What if I got lost in there and couldn't find my way out? I had no awareness at the time that I was the *observer* of my thoughts, not the thoughts themselves. And the observer always knows the way out.

Despite these aversions, I could no longer ignore what every therapist and book on anxiety was telling me about the benefits of meditation, not to mention thousands of years of precedent. So, despite not feeling physically or mentally ready—which may have taken forever—I started experimenting with it.

I first dipped my toes into the shallow end with Jack Kornfield. I ordered more CDs—Meditation for Beginners—and just listened, no meditating.

He described a practice that welcomed the inevitable thoughts that arise during meditation. He suggested picturing them on a small piece of paper above your head that then ignites into a small flame and floats away. One day, after listening to most of the CDs, he finally said, "Now let's close our eyes," and so I did. Unfortunately, I was driving at the time. I finally found the courage to let go and meditate in the middle of the highway. Luckily, I was sitting in stop-and-go traffic, so the honking horns brought me back to reality, and I continued on my way.

Jack was my gateway drug—I actually started sitting in silence, alone with my thoughts. While I felt some sense of success as I reported back to my therapist how many minutes I had strung together, I was also struck by the sense of failure it brought. How could something that had been proven to be a source of limitless benefits make me feel so horrible about myself?

Once I was actually able to sit for 10 minutes, I resolved to meditate daily. I failed immediately and then resolved to find my way to my mat as much as possible. When I did sit, despite Jack's suggestion, I couldn't light matches fast enough to keep up with all the lists, plans, and conversations that flurried through my mind. I was stuck in a loop of having the thoughts and then judging myself for them. I assumed it meant I was failing. I mean, if Jack suggested lighting them on fire, they couldn't be good, right? In reality, it meant I was a human meditating. But I didn't understand that at the time, so most days, I completely avoided it.

So how did I finally incorporate something into my life that made me feel like such a failure?

When sometime in my early 40s, I finally realized that my judgment was the failure, not the mat. So, I returned and tried over and over again.

I started with Oprah & Deepak's 21-Day Meditation Experiences. They provided accountability and focus. Each experience had a theme, and each day had a lesson that built from week to week. The meditations were posted daily and only available for five days. This gave me a sense of urgency when I first started. I knew that continuity in the lessons would create consistency. They also provided a mantra related to the daily lesson, which kept me focused (despite the fear of forgetting or mispronouncing it).

I became more convinced that this place of peace could be a reality when I listened to a lecture by Deepak Chopra called "The Modern Meditator," where he described what is now my favorite meditation metaphor. It gave me hope that I could manifest this peace and tap into it wherever and whenever I wanted or needed to. It was like the safety I felt at the waterfall, but now it wasn't just in my imagination; it was actually inside of me.

My version of it goes like this: When I am living my daily life, I am stuck in my head here on Earth, with thoughts of mostly the future ("to do" lists, "what if" thinking) and the past (judgment, shame) swirling through like the weather. Gone unchecked, this translates into a fear and ego-based existence that perpetuates anxiety.

The sun is the "Source." Our source of well-being, love, comfort, and peace. The Source is from where we came and where we will return. What the Source actually represents (God, the Universe, the Divine Unknown) is up to you. During our daily lives, it is mostly cloudy with a chance of grace. That grace comes when the clouds break a bit, and we feel the sun on our face and the Source touches our soul without us asking for it, being deserving of it, or meditating to find it.

When I sit and meditate, I imagine rising above the Earth and pushing through those clouds—like flying through clouds in a plane. It's dark and bumpy in there, and I never know what to expect. This is where the thoughts come in, the judgment, the itchy back, the hope that the timer goes off. But if I push through, the turbulence stops, and there is sunshine just above those clouds. And in meditation, there is clarity, calm, and peace just beyond those thoughts.

As I sit in the rays of the sun, connecting to the Source, those things that define me as a human being, those labels we adopt—wife, sister, stepmom, lawyer, writer, whatever they may be—fade away, and I connect with a deeper knowing and an expanded awareness that I believe to be my authentic self, my spiritual essence. It restores my memory of wholeness and connection to everything. Here, I find a calm and a sense of safety that I never knew existed within me because I could not remember living without fear.

Then the bell rings and I return to Earth and open my eyes, each time with the memory of those gifts I found just above the clouds in the presence of the Source. I can then tap into that sense of peace and connection as the memory grows stronger over time with repetition and practice.

This new reservoir of peace and empowerment emboldened me to step outside my box and test the waters. I knew that the safe place I had been running to my entire life was always right inside me, and that gave me the courage to do things I would have never thought possible. I took it on planes, boats, public transportation, and to parties. I drove it through tunnels, over bridges, on long road trips, and even on racetracks. I skied and ran long distances with it. I enjoyed movies, concerts, and plays with it. Most importantly, I opened my heart to true love with it. The fog lifted and the clouds parted as my life unfolded in front of my eyes. It blossomed into a world around me that expanded into limitless possibility.

But I still needed to make those possibilities a reality. Finding true freedom would mean living outside of my box forever. When I asked Martha Beck if that was possible, she gave me a meditation that I wished I'd had at the very beginning. This is where to start...

She told me to picture a wild, unbroken horse in a ring running tirelessly in circles ... running, running, running. She told me to picture every detail (like the jungle)—asking what I could see, hear, smell, and feel. She told me to do this meditation every day, noticing how all of those things change over time. She said that eventually, the horse would get tired and stop running, but to sit with it as the observer and watch it run for as long as it took—days, weeks, months even.

The first time I did it, I saw the horse through the wooden slats of the ring. I was wearing jeans and cowboy boots. The sun warmed my face, and a slight breeze slid over the grassy field. I heard the pounding of hooves on the hard dirt synchronized with the beat of my heart. Boom, boom. Boom, boom.

A cloud of dirt hovered just over the ground, lagging behind the horse's legs. It took my eyes a minute to catch up to him, but when they did, they never came off. His black hair glistened in the sun, and his muscles burst through his skin. He ran with the fear and pain I felt bursting through my own.

Like that horse, I felt alone in my struggle with this condition while navigating the pain it caused. Everyone was on the outside of the ring looking in and unable to help. I had no way to exhaust or extinguish the decades of pain stored inside me.

For weeks, I watched it run tirelessly in circles, transferring my negative emotions into the pounding of those hooves. Bit by bit, I felt them release with each lap he ran. Over time, I gained a sense of separation, unclenching my hands from the wooden fence rails and moving further away until I was hovering somewhere over the ring, listening to the pounding hooves from a distance.

Then one day, it stopped. The horse let out a snort of exhaustion and slowed to a trot and then a walk. It shook its head and then looked at me. I felt a sense of peace deep inside me. It was then that I began to believe that I may be able to cultivate and live in that place as an alternative to living in a constant state of anxiety. That possibility became real to me.

This meditation provided a great sense of relief on my journey. It gave me space to both metabolize my anxiety and find compassion for myself. What I had scratched the surface of on the plane to Ecuador and under the table with Estrella was now grounded in this practice, giving it space to take root and grow.

As my practice grew and my journey continued, my meditations started manifesting the healing I was searching for. One profound experience was when I was meditating on where I was always running to when I had panic attacks. Was I running from the box or back to it? Had my true self always been waiting for me on the outside?

I was very focused on clearing my mind and not trying to put the pieces of the puzzle together. My centering thought was, "I radiate complete peace and security." The Sanskrit mantra was "Om Bhu" (I express my stability into the world). I made no connections between the centering thought or mantra and the answers I was hoping to find. I just closed my eyes, cleared my mind, focused on my breath, and repeated the mantra.

When my mind wandered, I recentered, repeating the mantra silently while soft, meditative music played. Then I heard them—birds chirping faintly in the background. In an instant, I was back in the apartment I shared with Greg. I was hovering over my bed, looking down at myself wearing headphones. I was listening to the guided relaxation recording from MCAD.

I remembered how those few moments of peace before bed each night gave me hope during that dark time—hope that I wouldn't be a prisoner of my anxiety forever and that peace could be my reality.

Those birds chirping so many years later transported me back to that room. I lay next to her, hovering just above the bed, and held her hand. With each exhale, I felt more deeply connected to her, as if she were pulling me in and needing something I had.

Overwhelmed with emotion, I withdrew to witness what was happening for a moment and watched us on the bed from above. But within moments, she pulled me back in.

"Don't leave me," she said. I let go of my resistance and softened into the moment. As I lay there next to her, I looked up and saw the crack in the ceiling was still there. The apartment was the same, but I was drastically different than this woman beside me. Still holding her hand, I comforted her with the peace and security that I had finally found within myself. I felt her feel it. I felt us healing in that very moment. I had gone back to give her the treasure I had mined deep within myself.

When the soft bell rang to end the meditation, her hand tightened so as to not let me go. I struggled to open my eyes at first. I felt her begging me not to leave her. I squeezed her hand and said, "I will never leave you. We are one now. I am taking you home, and you will never be alone again." I opened my eyes and wept.

Meditations like that gave me a place to process and make sense of my pain, to find my broken pieces and put them back together.

Another came a few weeks before the second anniversary of my mother's death. I sat to do a typical daily meditation with Oprah & Deepak. This particular series was called Manifesting Grace through Gratitude, and the centering thought for the day was that as you put gratitude out into the world, grace flows back to you. The Sanskrit mantra was Twam Eva Mata, which means "The Universe is our mother."

I closed my eyes and started repeating the mantra slowly as music played in the background. I heard water flowing and the strings of a soft guitar. And then I heard them again—the birds. They sang, and suddenly, I found myself on the edge of the pool in a jungle where the waterfall emptied. It was my waterfall, but this time I wasn't alone. I was sitting in a circle of women in their 20s and 30s. I didn't recognize them at first. There was a light glowing around them. The woman on my left reached her hand into the water and dripped it over my forehead, softly pushing my bangs out of the way. I hadn't worn bangs since the second grade.

Then the woman next to her reached into the pool and poured another handful of water over my forehead—and then the next and the next, as if they were baptizing me. It was a spiritual cleansing of the pain I had processed. It felt redemptive. I couldn't tell the difference between the water flowing from my forehead and the tears streaming from my eyes. The last woman was on my right—it was my mother. She had been sitting there all along. Once I recognized her, I looked again at all of the other faces in the circle and saw my maternal and paternal grandmothers and realized the women I didn't recognize were their mothers and their mother's mothers.

My mother then cupped her hand in the pool and lifted it to my forehead, letting the water wash over me. Then she kissed the spot between my bangs where each baptism had been made. Then the soft bell rang to end the meditation, and the thought of leaving them was unbearable.

"We are always with you. We'll be right here by the waterfall whenever you want to return."

Then the circle of light grew so bright I could hardly see their faces. I opened my eyes and wiped my soaked cheeks. Looking up, I saw water droplets streaming down the window in front of me.

While I sat by that waterfall and those women baptized me in an eternal source of strength and love, while tears washed across my face releasing years of shame and pain, the heavens opened, and it began to rain.

The next time I found my way back to the waterfall, I felt plugged into something immediately. The light was neither bright nor dim; there was no activity, only a message.

"Look at that waterfall and that pool. Those are your tears. They create boundless power as they fall and collect into a pool that is an endless source of peace. Do not ask why they flow. Just know that here your pain finds a home and has a purpose."

Those meditations made me whole again and created a deep connection to the part of me that is eternal. They were an essential part of my journey—providing a place to heal, find reconciliation and redemption. They were not hours long or done in an ashram. They were 15 minutes, alone in my bedroom. And they certainly didn't happen every time I meditated. But they kept me coming back to my mat for more.

With each meditation like this, a new connection was made in the constellation—expanding my awareness and revealing the picture of my true self.

Chapter 33

The Crucible

"Your task is not to seek love, but merely to
seek and find all the barriers within yourself
you have built against it."
—Rumi

THE TRAJECTORY OF my decline into debilitating anxiety, the height
and thickness of the walls of my box, and my subsequent ascension
out was greatly affected by the relationships I had at the time and the
partners I chose.

My first husband was a kind and loving man, but he lived
in a bubble where no one talked about their fears, insecurities,
or mistakes. Everything was ignored, glossed over, and excused
with equanimity. This was accomplished by the incredible feat of
simultaneously having one's head in the clouds while also stuck
in the sand.

At the time, I thought I was in control, and I could protect anyone from my condition. But that's never the case. The people you let into your life will either add fuel to the fire or carry buckets of water to help put out the flames.

My current husband, David, was exactly the opposite. He didn't understand anxiety either but asked the questions I should have been asking myself all along. And by the time we met, my awareness had expanded. I was aware of my box and already testing its boundaries. The limitations I still needed to overcome were very clear. I was also in a much more empowered place where I was no longer willing to hide my anxiety or protect others from it.

"Whatever you do, don't hug me." It was our second date, and I raised my first warning flag. It was a level of vulnerability I still wasn't comfortable with. It barely registered for him. We were just starting out and confident that we would be together forever, so we had time to explore my boundaries. And we did.

For me, a hug was something I longed for as a child. I thought it would make me feel accepted for exactly who I was and loved unconditionally, beyond measure. But I had no recollection of such hugs or feelings, only a hole still waiting to be filled. That would require walls to come crashing down, exposing me to feelings I wasn't ready for yet, so I drew a line in the sand. The thought of those walls falling was too overwhelming to consider.

It would take time for me to allow myself to feel what waited for me on the other side. I allowed myself the space to step toward it and the hope to consider it. And he walked that path alongside me.

His love and support motivated me to do the work—to try without knowing the outcome and expose myself to intense feelings of shame and worthlessness and walk through the fire together. Well, sort of. Sometimes we walked through together, and sometimes I went through it alone. But I always found him waiting for me on the other side. He did it all without judgment, resentment, or anger. The more space he gave, the more I exposed myself, finding the courage to move through it and find myself beyond it. With him, escaping my box finally seemed like a real possibility.

I was already on my journey out of the box, so when he reached out his hand to help lift me to the other side, I grabbed hold with everything I had. I saw the light at the end of the tunnel in his eyes.

Once the house sold and my divorce was final, I moved in with my sister in New Hampshire. I commuted to Boston on a bus for two hours each way. I left on the 6:30 a.m. and, if I was lucky, took the 7:30 p.m. home. I worked in my office alone all day, rarely talking to anyone except to order lunch. It isn't typical for lawyers in law firms to socialize throughout the day, given the billable hour requirements. When I arrived back at the bus terminal each night, I drove straight to an empty gym and worked out until closing. Sleep, wake up at 5 a.m., repeat.

Over time, I knew the bus drivers and recognized the same commuters every day. Some of us became close enough to socialize on weekends. After a year of this, I realized how small my world had become. I was going in the wrong direction.

"If I don't make a drastic change, I will never meet anyone but the 30 people on this bus," I thought.

The routine was creating another box I was suffocating in, so when one of my clients posted an opening for an in-house counsel position, I jumped at the chance. On my first day there, the head of Human Resources walked me to each office, introducing me to everyone. When we reached David's office, his eyes never left his computer screen as she introduced me and explained what I would be doing there.

"Counsel?" he asked, finally looking up to make eye contact with her.

"Yes," she replied. "If there's anything you …"

"I don't use lawyers. We won't be working together… at all." He shifted his eyes to me as he delivered the "at all."

"But good luck," he said abruptly, looking back at his monitor.

"OK, then." I smiled awkwardly at Human Resources and checked the "no need to remember *his* name" box in my head.

We wouldn't actually see or hear each other again for almost two years. And I don't mean see with our eyes and hear with our ears, because we worked right down the hall from each other. I mean *really* see and *really* hear, with our heart and our souls.

Once our paths did cross, it was as if we were meeting for the first time and had known each other forever all at once, and that was it. Simultaneously, we each reached out our hands to each other, and together, we danced. He became the catalyst that would have me both willfully shed my fear of vulnerability and break my heart open to authentic love and a deep connection that was not possible inside my box.[21]

Before him, my anxious mind had experienced romantic relationships by imagining the worst-case scenarios and dwelling on them so long that my brain believed they actually happened. These painful memories had paralyzed me with fear, twisted my thoughts, and created a reality that never actually happened. For all I knew, every boyfriend had cheated on me in every way possible, fathered children with other women, led double lives on the Internet, were in the Witness Protection Program, and stayed with me only because they secretly thought I was too unstable to leave.

As a result, I became even more vigilant with each new relationship, and the panic attacks became more intense and unpredictable. These walls were some of my highest and strongest because I started building them when I watched my parents' relationship. From inside that box, I listened as pointed questions turned to blame, and sharp words amplified to yelling. I watched as faces turned red and eyes filled with tears. I saw dishes hit walls, vitamins cover floors, cabinets slam, and doors get kicked in. I cried as my father attempted to hold her and calm the rage, only to be turned into a punching bag. I tried to negotiate a truce during the weeks of silence that followed. I wondered each day if he would come home from work to save me or save himself and leave me there alone. But he always returned, with flowers sometimes, only to her disgust, and his tears broke me.

In David, I found a man who didn't offer to put me back together. He didn't swim me across that channel of despair. We both knew I would have to do that myself. He sat patiently on the other side, and with all of my fears, insecurities, and shame exposed, he whispered in my ear, "You are loved. You are powerful beyond measure. You are deserving of every dream you have ever had." He reminded me of that voice inside me that had been silenced by early traumas, years of angst, and decades of anxiety. And he gave me a buoy to swim to.

"Crucible" is defined as a situation of severe trial or a situation in which concentrated forces or different elements interact, causing change and leading to the creation of something new.[22] This relationship was my crucible. The trials unfolded as the forces and different elements we each brought to the relationship interacted. They challenged us to change the dance by creating a new harmony.

By way of mental and emotional context, I grew up ashamed of my body and sexual appetite. I grew up Catholic. I had sex in the dark, not only to hide my physical flaws but because if God were watching, maybe he wouldn't recognize me without the lights on. I was taught the road to hell was paved with lustful thoughts, so I couldn't even watch R-rated films with nudity and sexual content without jumping out of my skin and into a confessional. As a result, I struggled with the conflicting feelings of shame and the desire for physical contact and satisfaction.

One of the first trials I remember was on an unassuming Sunday afternoon soon after we'd started our relationship. I found myself lying on top of the bed wearing only underwear and a bra, anticipating sex. When David walked in, I asked if he could close the blinds, draw the drapes, and maybe get some masking tape to fill in any cracks where sunlight could peek through. Instead, he smiled, removed his clothes, and lay on top of the covers next to me.

"How about you just lie here naked with me instead. No sex. Just hold my hand, listen to the music, and trust me."

"What the fuck!" my brain screamed so loud I was sure he heard it. The sudden rush of adrenaline and intense fear were almost more than I could handle. It was the saber-toothed tiger I had been expecting my entire anxious life. My breath quickened, and my heart raced. I felt flush in the face and feared my palms would start to sweat, making the "hold hands" request a non-starter.

I rolled off the bed and whispered, "I'll be right back," as I slipped into the bathroom. I grabbed the sides of the sink and looked at myself in the mirror. I scanned my body and took a deep breath.

The nudity was a level of exposure I was not sure I could handle. It was like a hug—it crossed some imaginary line of intense discomfort. It went far beyond exposing the private places I had been hiding since that day in the fort. It would reveal every flaw, imperfection, and questionable grooming choice to a man I adored. It was counterintuitive to my anxious brain that was screaming, "Hide! Run!" The vulnerability was terrifying. My flight response was in overdrive.

The window behind me was too high to crawl out of, and the rest of my clothes were still in the bedroom. I paced back and forth, reminding myself that if I was going to find my way out of this box and open myself to a love I'd not been capable of while in it, I would have to say "yes" while my mind was screaming "no."

So, with my heart still beating wildly, I unhooked my bra and slid my panties off past my shaking knees. As I opened the door, my sweaty palm slipped off the knob. "Shit!" I thought, and my heart sank. When I re-entered the bedroom, he wasn't sitting up glaring at the door waiting for me. He sensed my discomfort, so he just lay there still as I climbed onto the bed next to him. His hand rolled onto mine, and I slid my fingers through his.

"Sorry about the sweat," I said.

"Shhhh. Just listen."

I clenched my eyes closed, breathed deeply in through my nose, then exhaled the overwhelm.

Then Sting sang to me.

> "She looked beneath her shirt today.
> There was a wound in her flesh so deep and wide.
> From the wound a lovely flower grew
> From somewhere deep inside.
> She turned around to face her mother
> To show her the wound in her breast that burned like a brand.
> But the sword that cut her open
> Was the sword in her mother's hand.
>
> Every day another miracle
> Only death will tear us apart
> To sacrifice a life for yours
> I'd be the blood of the Lazarus heart...
> The wound itself would give her power
> The power to remake herself
> At the time of her darkest hour.
> She said the wound would give her courage and pain
> The kind of pain that you can't hide
> From the wound a lovely flower grew
> From somewhere deep inside."[23]

This was the first of many moments along our journey that ranged from discomfort and unease to overwhelming anxiety and terror. My fears started with, "What if I'm just not able to break down these walls, and I never find my way out? What if I'm broken forever? Then he cheats or leaves me?" They morphed into, "What if I break down my walls and give this 100% and I *am* enough. What if it is everything I've ever wanted, and then he cheats or leaves?"

At the time, I felt mentally prepared for the first scenario, but the second would be excruciating, and I wasn't sure I could recover from it. The fear then became, "What if I can never give of myself completely and be fully present and emotionally available in this relationship?"

If that was my mindset, I would never grow, and this would never work. I could blame and run, seeking short-term relief from intense discomfort while killing something deep inside me. Stepping back toward my box wasn't an option when I looked into his eyes and saw our future.

Sitting in front of him during difficult conversations, completely terrified, he pushed and pulled me in ways that challenged me to see the excess stone still obstructing the sculpture we were trying to reveal together. I would look at the chisel lying on the table between us and praying for the strength and courage to pick it up.

As I sat in the fire, facing my fiercest demons, the pressure built, peeling back the layers until the shame was exposed and I spoke my truth, my deepest fears, regardless of how irrational. I didn't know what I would find when I chipped away at what no longer served me. The pieces hit the floor, splashing into a puddle of tears, revealing places in me that had never been exposed to the light. And he met me there, supporting my brave choices and reciprocating. Each of these conversations was a crucible, taking our relationship to a new, deeper level and profoundly changing me in the process.

In these challenging situations, the stronger the fear and anxiety pulsed through my veins, the more important it was to stay and not run. Those are the choices that transform you. Only through revealing your true self can you find true connection. Listen with courage when your soul cries for more, and lean into the spaces that terrify you.

After over 10 years together, what I've learned is that finding that deep connection was essential to finding my way out of my box, and vice versa. The crucible created something and someone new. Over time I became more aware of situations that would trigger the "old me," so I started seeking out opportunities to put my feet in the fire and do the work prophylactically. In exercising this muscle, the confrontations become less frequent.

I also learned that when you find the person who is willing to meet you where you are, breaking down your walls does not expose you to heartbreak and abandonment. When you are met with this crucible, the metamorphosis fundamentally changes you. You believe in your worthiness and find self-love.

For me, this meant two things. First, you become more attractive to everyone, not just physically but on every level, because you now own your divine individuality. Therefore, you are less likely to be abandoned or betrayed. And second, even if you *are* abandoned or betrayed, you now know that their actions expose who they are, not who you are. It becomes impossible to be broken by it. Will it be painful? Of course. But you are unattached to the result, not because you don't care, but because you know you will be OK no matter what happens.

Ironically, falling in love with someone else gave me the ability to fall in love with myself. I was draped in a lightness of being, and I delighted in my unique qualities. These gifts were always within me, hidden by the stone that I could only remove when challenged by a longing so deep it became impossible to ignore. That's what true love can do.

Part 4

LIVING OUTSIDE THE BOX

The River

It's been so long now I don't remember how I got here or where I was before. I sit by the river bank all day, taking in the beauty of the jungle that surrounds me. Vines drape from tree to tree like streamers, creating connections above ground that are usually only found deep below the surface. Lily pads lay beautifully buoyant, decorating the surface of the water. They come into my life only briefly and then travel on to wherever the river takes them.

Drops of water sit on glistening leaves above me then slide off into the river, becoming one with it. While I can't quite place what I'm longing for, I feel a palpable emptiness and envy them all.

Turning away from my thoughts, I find comfort in the sun warming my face and joy in the distant sound of birds singing. But even in the safety, I also feel a deep sense of loneliness. I forget who I left behind, but remember just enough that I am saddened at the thought. I sit at the river's edge, wondering where the water came from and where it's going. Its journey feels vaguely familiar, but I fear I will never know.

I doze into a half slumber and hear what sounds like a child singing in the distance. I let the notes float gently across my ears and settle in my soul, not knowing if I am dreaming or if it's real. As it grows closer, I realize it's not singing at all, but fearful whimpering. I open my eyes and see a girl hopping quickly from one lily pad to the next, trying to stay above the water's surface. Her arms are stretched out wide to keep her balance. She looks exhausted and terrified, as if she sees things in the water that frighten her or fears she might fall in and drown.

I try to walk closer, quietly so I won't startle her, but a stick breaks under my feet. She looks up suddenly, loses her balance, and splashes into the water. Holding my breath, I wait for her to surface but see no sign. In a moment, I know I could never sit on this bank again and find any sense of solitude without knowing what's happened to her. If I thought she had died because I didn't save her, something inside me would die, too. I dive in without knowing what will happen or what I will find.

The water is beautifully clear, and I find her fully submerged. I swim under her and lift her to the surface on my back. When I open my eyes, it is dark as night. The water has turned to ink with only the lily pads lit up by the moon's glow. Creatures I can't identify slither around us.

With a ferocious cough, she comes to and grips me tightly. In that moment, I know I am seeing the jungle through her eyes.

My chest tightens, and my limbs weaken as panic sets in. The weight of her on my back becomes too much for me to stay afloat. Just before the water overtakes us, she slides off me and we roll onto our backs. In that moment, drained of all energy and strength, I hold her hand and completely let go of the struggle to stay afloat. With each slow, deep breath, our bodies become more buoyant, the darkness fades, the creatures disappear, and the water becomes clear again. She turns her head to look at me, and I know she is now seeing through my eyes.

In our grasp, I can no longer tell where I end and she begins. I feel at one with the water as it lifts and carries us further downstream than I've ever seen from my spot on the riverbank. Now I will finally experience where this river can take me.

Chapter 34

Finding Fulfillment in Failure

"I have not failed. I've just found 10,000 ways
that won't work."
—Thomas A. Edison

I'M SURE YOU'VE HEARD the saying, "What would you do if you knew
you couldn't fail?" I can think of lots of things, thousands even. I
would sing the national anthem at the Super Bowl. I would fly a
fighter jet and land it on an aircraft carrier. I would dance on tour
with Lady Gaga.

But what is the point if that is not reality? I think the intent behind
the exercise is to uncover the big dreams that are hidden behind our
fear of failure. Isn't dreaming big still just dreaming if we don't recognize failure is always possible? When we realize that possibility, our
list shrinks, but if you are willing to fail, the list expands and gets more
interesting. And what if you take it one step further?

What would you do if you knew you were going to fail and facing failure would change you—maybe slightly over time, or profoundly in an instant? What moves you so strongly that your fear of failure takes a backseat to what you are compelled to do? When do you know in your heart that shrinking from a challenge, again, will leave you feeling so miserable that diving in and failing will actually bring fulfillment?

How many times have you been convinced you are going to fail at something, walked away, and beat yourself up knowing that was the wrong choice? I can't count how many times I've done that. Fear and anxiety are too often our focus rather than our fuel—our roadblock rather than our guidepost. Once we convince ourselves we are going to fail, what if we see the fear and anxiety as signs pointing us in the direction we need to go, the path of our authentic journey, and choose to do it while afraid and anxious? What if we bring fear and anxiety along for the ride?

Not only are we exhilarated by such a brave choice, but we are fundamentally changed by what happens when we face a challenge despite our perceived limitations and nonattachment to the outcome. Without challenge, there is no change.

Not only do we challenge the capacity of our courage, but we challenge our definitions of success and failure, leading to new experiences that are so much more than an exercise in accumulating accomplishments or collecting adventures. They stoke the fires of metamorphosis, breaking down walls, creating space for and giving life to our authentic selves.

There are a thousand ways to fail. You can fail big, or you can slightly miss the mark. Be willing to do, even master, both. Be more willing to challenge your story of how you've failed in the past and what failure looks and feels like now. To be clear, I am in no way saying that you should try to fail. I am not suggesting that you give less than your all, whatever that may be at the time, to see what failure feels like. I'm saying recognize when you believe failure is most certain and your fear feels too strong to overcome, but you hear a whisper—or maybe a scream—suggesting you take that path anyway. Rather than turn a deaf ear or have one foot in and one foot out, you dive in wholeheartedly.

This is what I asked myself over and over again. I would have to find a new relationship with failure. It had to become a welcome companion. Here is how I found my way through it:

Recognize the Signs: Begin to see fear as fuel rather than yet another failure. Fear and anxiety can be reactions that guide you to exactly where you want to be. When given two choices, one challenging and one safe, I feel it instantly. Something stirs deep inside me, my mind starts racing, and sometimes my eyes start tearing because in that moment, I feel the power of that choice. Will I shrink back to safety, or will I move through the fear of failure, lack, and hurt, and open myself to discover who I am on the other side? Those tears are surely tears of fear, but not the fear of the challenge. Those tears are from the fear that I will make the safe choice again, which I know will be my greatest failure and will cause the most painful lack, the lack of fulfillment.

Play it out: Fear and anxiety are fueled by the stories we tell ourselves. "Failure is embarrassing, defining even. People will see me struggle and judge me. People will discover I'm a fraud. Failure exposes my imperfection, making me unlovable." The only way to change that story is to play it out in real life and change the ending. Find out what really happens when you fail. Get to know the person who exposed herself, knowing there was likely pain and failure and embarrassment ahead. Feel the connection to others that comes from those experiences. Recognize your role as the writer of your story and start changing the ending, page by page.

Expand Your Horizons: Failure can look and feel far different than what we've been telling ourselves all these years. The more we experience it, the more comfortable we are with it. We learn that we are not defined by our failures but by our choices to show up and challenge ourselves. We learn that we don't fail as much as we thought we would. We learn that our traditional definitions of failure no longer have a place in our story. Then the limits, the boundaries, and the walls that the fear of failure built over so many years come crumbling down, and our lives become limitless.

Choosing to act despite the possibility or likelihood of failure will make you a bigger success than you ever dreamed.

Moment's Reprieve

Oh! beautiful day, beautiful skies
lifting my head and opening my eyes

without any effort I start to smile
seems it's been waiting here all the while.

Oh! glorious night, glorious moon
sleep will have me dreaming soon

the thought of ending this day brings tears
the day I forgot all of my fears.

Chapter 35

Beyond the Break

*"Nature holds countless lessons if we are only still enough
to observe and absorb."*
—Me

JUST BEFORE THE storm hit, I sat in a window seat and watched winter ducks float effortlessly in the frigid water. The ocean was angry, anticipating the storm.

"How would I be acting right now if I were a duck?" I thought.

From the inside of my box, I would have been panicking and swimming for shore (with floaties on both arms). At the very least, I would be wading very close to the edge so I could get out at a moment's notice.

But as the winds began to howl, they remained unfazed. They didn't fear blowing away because they knew they could fly. And even with the storm building, they floated along completely calm and confident.

As the waves climbed higher and crashed ferociously around them, they didn't fly away or float to the shore. They did exactly the opposite, the unexpected. They moved further out into the ocean to a calm spot just beyond the break.

It was a place I could never get to from inside the box because I was too afraid to move toward a wave and discover what awaited me on the other side. I spent my life either bracing for the crash or retreating to safer ground. If only I'd known that if I released my grip, cut my tether, and moved just beyond my comfort zone, I could ride the wave rather than be destroyed by it. If only I'd known that if I leaned into my fears for just long enough to spread my wings, the air that once assaulted me would support me and lift me to new heights. If only …

The next day when the storm was over, I looked out the window to find the same ducks—still floating, still calm, still ducks.

Still reminding me that my circumstances don't dictate my life, my thoughts and reactions to them do. The waves may break, but I don't have to. If I move toward the wave despite my fear and embrace the challenge it presents, I develop the confidence and courage to ride it to its crest and either float through to the calm on the other side or spread my wings and fly.

That's when the world becomes a playground rather than a battlefield. It embraces me rather than beats me down. It supports and sustains me rather than depletes and destroys me.

All of that peace and power was always waiting for me, just beyond the break.

Chapter 36

The Gears (Never Say Never)

*"Be a learner first, a master second,
and a student always."*
—Ernie J. Zelinski

LEARNING HOW TO DRIVE A CAR with a manual transmission may seem insignificant, but we are not presented with a hero's journey every day. Every choice counts; every promise kept, every lesson learned either moved me forward or pulled me back. I had to ask myself daily, "Am I making this choice based on my own terms or based on fear? Is my choice pulling me out of my comfort zone or reinforcing my walls? Do my choices align with my spiritual path? "

It's never about the shiny sports car, but rather who is in the driver's seat and in which direction they are going. It's about the barriers we build between who we are and who we want to be.

When I bought my dream car (it was used—I recycled), I dove in headfirst because the barrier was clear, and the resistance was immediate. And while I knew it presented a challenge, I underestimated the lessons I'd learn from stepping that far out of my comfort zone.

The car appeared within minutes of starting my search, as if it was meant to be. The catch was that it had a six-speed manual transmission, and I had never driven a stick. In fact, I'd purposefully avoided it.

"I will *never* do that. It makes no sense. I don't want to think about actually driving; I just want to get there. *And* I have panic attacks all the time while driving, so what happens then? How would I do both? Never."

I claimed I had no desire despite desperately wanting to drive my husband's shiny, manual transmission sports cars. The truth was that I was terrified of being judged, feeling out of control, looking foolish, quitting, and ultimately failing. As a result, I chose the passenger's seat rather than the driver's seat, justifying the decision in my head while my gut felt uneasy, embarrassed, and even ashamed.

Now, the possibility of having this car was suddenly real, but it came at a cost that wasn't included in the price tag. I could have looked a little harder and found an automatic with less appeal and more miles, but I knew the time had come to face this fear. The decision wasn't just about owning this car or even driving the others anymore; it was about facing the resistance and moving through it. It was about recognizing the fabricated limitations and identifying the story in my head as false. So, I bought the car, the uncertain outcome, and the possibility of looking foolish and failing. I bought it all because even if I failed and traded the car in for an automatic, I knew that in the *trying*, I was breaking down barriers and moving further outside my box.

While I shouted my lack of confidence from the rooftops, David constantly reassured me, "You can totally do it! Look at all the people in the world who can drive a manual." He was right. We identified a few, and I thought of them often. In situations like these, it's sometimes helpful to look to people who are the exact opposite of your strong and courageous role model. Those people with no common sense or coordination can be just as inspiring. You remember them and think, *If they can do it, then of course, I can do it.*

Ultimately, I not only learned how to drive a six-speed manual, but I learned six important lessons that help me stay out of my box and will serve me far longer than this car ever will.

First Gear: Say "Yes" to Firsts

"Firsts" are uncomfortable because they are unpredictable. As we get older and make our own choices (hopefully!), it's less likely that we say "yes" to something we've never experienced before. And the more we shy away from them, the more we forget how to navigate them.

We build resistance rather than resilience.

But if you keep saying "yes," it can open up the world. Every time we say "yes" to another first, we become more comfortable with all that comes with it—the trepidation, the questions, the fear and panic. They become so repetitive that after a while, we say, "I've felt that before," or "That voice sounds familiar," or "Here we go again (eye roll)." The more we stop overthinking, push through, and take action, the more positive outcomes we experience and can pull from the next time we are faced with a first.

Over time, as our confidence grows, we become more and more open to trying new things and more resilient to the fear of unpredictable outcomes and failure.

"Yes" is more than a word. It's an investment in what is possible.

Second Gear: Make a Decision and Commit

If you shift into first gear, release the clutch, and don't apply enough gas, you will stall. You made the decision, but if there is something holding you back, even subconsciously, you will never gain momentum. Similarly, if you have one foot on the gas but the other is still pressing the clutch, you have not fully engaged a gear, and there will be no progress until you figure out why that foot is still on the clutch. Find a gear and commit fully. And if you feel resistance, commit to doing the work to uncover what's holding you back, and then recommit to moving forward. Only then can you follow your path.

Third Gear: Don't Focus on Your Past to Determine What You are Capable of in the Future

If you stalled in first and struggled to find second, keep moving forward to third. Your heart may be ready to change gears, but your brain will fight you in ways that may be hard to see.

Our brain is built for survival—to seek instant gratification, immediate comfort, and resist change and challenge. It also likes to prove itself right. That's why you hear your saboteurs say, "See? I told you so. I knew you would fail."

Don't listen! Don't look to your past to determine what you are capable of in the future. Don't believe your brain when it interprets your failures as evidence that you can't achieve something. Those failures just mean you are closer than ever to achieving your goal.

When the brain looks back for evidence that change and challenge are insurmountable obstacles and threats to our wellbeing, we fall into resistance and conflict with ourselves.

When we focus on the future and the calling in our heart that asks, "What is possible?" we tap into our curiosity and creativity. We are aligned with our purpose and find a deep sense of peace even in the discomfort of change. The question generates excitement and action rather than terror and paralysis.

Focused on the future, we consciously make ourselves available to tap into the universal power that is available when we have the courage and confidence to claim it. Focused on the past, we miss the doors that are opening all around us and never take the next step that reveals and illuminates our path.

Remember when you learned to walk or ride a bike? No one watched you fall 10 times and said, "Well, this child just isn't gonna get it." That's what your brain likes to say. Be the child with wide eyes and a wild heart, undeterred by the falls, confident that the next try may be the one!

Expect and embrace expansion even through the trial and error period. Keep dreaming. Keep looking forward. And keep believing that the Universe will rise up to catch you when you lean into the life you want to create.

Fourth Gear: Pay Attention and Be Ready to Pivot

In fourth gear, you are cruising. You may actually forget you are driving a manual. You might imagine your route home and the traffic and a hill start or two. But even if you have navigation, the reality is that you have no idea how any of it will play out. Why? Because you have no control over the other cars, when lights will change from green to red, when you will encounter a detour, or when someone will cross the street.

All of these things actually matter a *lot* when you are first learning to drive a manual transmission. You have to pay attention to everything unfolding around you and be able to pivot. If you panic, you'll stall. And that's fine, too. It will happen. So, pause, assess the surroundings, and start again.

Fifth Gear: Don't Make Decisions Based on Fear

I questioned my decision to make this major investment before learning how to drive it every day for those first four weeks. Every time I stalled in traffic or drove past a store because I didn't know how to parallel park, I thought, *What was I thinking? Why did I think this was a good idea again?*

On day 14, I started crying behind the wheel. I was anxious and beating myself up for putting myself in this situation. That old voice came back, asking, "Who did I think I was? We have anxiety; we can't do things like this."

Once home, I meditated, seeking clarity on what to do next. I thought about quitting. I struggled to imagine ever feeling comfortable driving this car. Then I heard a voice as loud and clear as I've ever heard anything.

"We do not make decisions based on fear."

Exactly. This was not a rash decision; it was the right decision. Sometimes having more time to consider a decision just gives us more time to rationalize saying "no." I bought that car quickly not because I forgot I had anxiety, but because I *remembered* I had anxiety, and I was ready to face it head-on. Anxiety was going to be there whether I bought the car or not. It seeps its way into every crevice and crack it can find. I would have anxiety in any car I bought, but the anxiety would have made that decision, not me.

Sixth Gear: Who is in the Driver's Seat?

Take a good hard look at who or what drives you through your days, your months, your life. Is it family and work obligations, addiction, family of origin wounds, trauma, anxiety, comparison to friends and neighbors? The list is long and most, if not all, share one common theme: *fear*. Fear of failure, fear of change, fear of lack, fear of loss, fear of letting go of that which no longer serves us. Of course, we all have obligations to our families, our employers, and friends, but these should not be shallow duties or relationships that turn us into slaves to schedules and consumerism. Take back the wheel and find your own, authentic path.

Ultimately, this wasn't an investment in a car; it was an investment in myself and my recovery. I was exercising the muscle of feeling foolish and failing to build up my tolerance to those uncomfortable feelings and the strength to act anyway.

Chapter 37

Never Say Never Again

*"Freeing yourself was one thing, claiming ownership
of that freed self was another."*
—Toni Morrison

"I WILL *NEVER* DO THAT. *Never.*" Buying that car was not the only time I said that. I said it A LOT. It made complete sense to me from inside my box. I knew my limitations and laughed at and ignored people who tried to talk me into doing things I told myself I couldn't handle. They didn't know the battles I'd fought and the war I had been waging for years. I had convinced myself that anything that challenged my sense of safety and control would end in tragedy.

Living outside my box would mean challenging my own thoughts and discerning between real and imagined danger. I needed to make decisions based on what I wanted, not what I thought I was capable of with anxiety. I needed to expose myself to the very experiences I'd imagine would kill me. I needed to rewrite the ending of those tragic stories my anxious mind replayed over and over. I needed to retrain my brain.

Those five words—*I will never do that*—became a signpost pointing me in the exact direction I needed to go.

When I heard myself say it, I'd pause and smile. I'd take a moment to listen to my story and identify the fear. Was it actually an inherently dangerous activity? Was I afraid of judgment or failure? Was my soul crying out for it? How does it feel in your body? Are you attracted to it or repelled by it?

Martha Beck calls this tracking—like tracking an animal. When you think about what you fear, does it feel like a cold track or a hot track? A cold track is aversion-based. Your soul isn't calling out for it, and your body recoils. This is the good kind of fear. A hot track is attraction-based. Something deep inside of you longs to lean in and your body stirs with excitement. While these sensations may feel similar to anxiety, this fear is only holding you back. This is a track you should most definitely follow.

Most of the time, the tracks of my fear were hot as hell. The next step was not to say "yes" and beat back the anxiety. It was to accept the anxiety and move toward my curiosity, toward the adventure, toward expanding rather than bracing and shrinking. It required me to remain open to and embrace all of my thoughts, feelings, and physical sensations and move through them to see who I was on the other side.

Out of my comfort zone, I sometimes found a quiet stillness that, at first, disturbed me simply because I wasn't used to it. It reminded me of a moment I once experienced following really terrible turbulence while descending through a storm cloud—suddenly, the plane jerked and became silky smooth. It was so still and unexpected I opened my eyes, looked at David, and asked, "Did we die?"

I reminded myself there was no place safer than where I was, and I already embodied all the power I could ever need. With this mindset, the possibilities seemed endless. My world expanded around me, and the gifts came pouring in—skiing, yoga, spinning, driving race cars, kayaking, camping, sailing, loving my husband completely, forgiving my mother, being a stepmom, and even writing.

Sailing

We bought a boat. Not a boat with a motor that stays upright in the wind and doesn't take on water. We bought a sailboat. She sits low in the water with beautiful lines. I said yes to this proposition, and as I heard the words coming out of my mouth, I heard a voice in my head saying, "This is a mistake of epic proportion. Take it back. Take it back!" But I didn't. I let the affirmation hang out there in space for a while to see how it affected my husband and my spirit. And at that moment, we became owners of a sailboat that would challenge my comfort zone in countless ways.

The summer before, we toyed with the idea of buying a powerboat while the kids were still young. When David suggested a sailboat instead, I promptly replied, "You can't afford the only type of sailboat I would sail on. It's big and has a bathroom and a motor. Otherwise, never. I could never be stuck out there at the whim of the elements with no place to go to the bathroom, no ability to get back to the harbor, no lifeline, no ripcord, never. Just the thought of it makes me anxious. I would never, *ever* do that."

Yet, here I was. The challenges began before we even bought it. It was late October, and we were scheduled to test drive the boat. It was the only boat left in the harbor.

I tried to look on the bright side—the sky was blue and … the sky was blue. The cons were more obvious to me than anyone else—the wind was howling, it was cold, I didn't know the person sailing this boat, and I was not a strong swimmer—not even in a pool, never mind the Atlantic Ocean.

Initially, I refused to go. I wasn't exercising my exposure muscle just yet. Eventually, I agreed to go to the dock and look at it, but wore knee-high leather barn boots with jeans, convinced that they would not allow me on the boat dressed like that. I knew there would be coaxing at the dock, and I didn't want to refuse and then cry as they sailed away, feeling inadequate and ashamed. I figured my inappropriate footwear alone would save me from that humiliation.

But to my surprise (and horror), the boots didn't get a second glance. Before I knew it, I was on the boat with four men, searching my pockets for a stray Klonopin. I came up empty. I would have to start believing I had everything I could ever need. I knew everyone on the boat knew more about sailing than I did, so I told myself, "*I won't panic until they panic.*" It was like watching the flight attendants when turbulence gets bad.

What I found was that when the boat heeled over (what I interpreted as tipping over and capsizing), my stomach dropped, and my knuckles turned white, no one else seemed alarmed. Apparently, that was sailing.

Under normal circumstances, I would have instinctively moved to the high side of the boat. But with four large men, there was no room to shift around. I was stuck there, deep in the exposure. So, I leaned into my discomfort, and I lay back. Yes, I actually lay back toward the water and watched the waves pass just under my head. I inhaled and closed my eyes. Typically, when I realized there was no way out, I would panic. Now I embraced it and found a strange sense of peace waiting for me on the other side.

What I've learned after three summers on the boat is that you cannot predict the outcome of any given sail. It is completely dependent on the weather, the seas, and the boat traffic, all of which are entirely out of my control and ever-changing. Despite checking every weather station and iPhone app, the wind is always different than forecasted. Like skiing, the sweet spot is amazing and precious because it is rare and fleeting. But it was in the moments around the sweet spot that I was challenged and grew the most.

At first, I helped prepare the boat for sail while still on the mooring. If it seemed too windy, I cried. It's difficult for people without anxiety to understand all the crying, but my brain was telling me that I would die—like flying, skiing, driving, etc. That elicits an emotional response and is challenging to process in the moment.

The paradox with sailing is that with no wind, you are rendered helpless, bobbing around in the water, praying for a puff. So too much was scary, and too little was miserable. I was uncomfortable with it all. My comfort zone was extremely small, reminiscent of my box. Staying in that box basically meant you never sailed, so it was not an option.

On one particularly windy day with choppy seas, we heeled over so far that I shouted, "I'll jump off this boat! I swear!" At first, it worked. David let out the sails slightly, and the boat straightened up a bit. But I've thought about that reaction many times since then. How would jumping into the ocean have made things better? I was on an enormous life raft, yet my panic just screamed "Run!"—even if that meant jumping in the ocean. My constant need to run or escape never appeared more irrational than in that moment. I had everything I needed on the boat.

My brain didn't look at a boat and see relaxation or adventure. My brain saw a boat and immediately recalled the day I was struck by the boom and tossed into the ocean and swallowed by the 5-foot waves. And the day my husband fell off the boat, and I was unable to sail around to him in time before he slipped below the surface and drowned. And the time the gusts grew so strong, the boat tipped over, tossing me into the water and pinning me under the sail, unable to breathe or find my way out from under it. And the day the forecast called for sun, and a storm suddenly struck, shedding the sails and sinking the boat with me on it.

Of course, none of those things actually happened, but I thought of them so often and so vividly that my subconscious didn't know the difference. Having new experiences on the boat where these horrible scenarios *didn't* happen was the exposure therapy I needed to create lasting change.

Skiing

In the book *What We Ache For,* Oriah Mountain Dreamer talks about lowering your expectations and asks what you are willing to do poorly. What do you do despite being bad at it?

"Everything I never did because I had anxiety," was my answer. I'm willing to do it all poorly, but I'm sure as hell going to do it because that's living outside my box. Had I responded from inside the box, my answer would have been, "Nothing. I am not willing to do anything poorly. If you reveal your imperfections to others, if you look foolish and fail, you are replaceable and unlovable." That was the fear and shame talking. Now, outside my box, I wasn't willing to stay inside to appear perfect and gain acceptance or love. I needed to be true to myself first. I needed to do it messy and anxious in order to respect and love myself at the end of each day.

Skiing made the top of the list. After my first attempt with my first husband in Utah, I didn't ski again until I met David. He had a house in Vermont perfectly situated within about an hour's drive of seven ski resorts. I don't recall how the conversation went, but I'm sure when asked, I overstated my abilities.

Our first ski outing was at Mad River Glen, whose slogan is "Ski It If You Can." This would take on different meanings for me over the years. Initially, I thought they were bragging about how difficult it was. "I can't, so let's find something easier," I thought. I didn't say it out loud, so I found myself walking through the parking lot awkwardly carrying my equipment and reading that slogan on every car's bumper sticker. It added to the pressure and fear that was already building, but once again, there was no turning back.

I hired an instructor for two hours, and once we reached the top of the double chair lift, I asked to start on the beginner slopes (green), to which she said, "We don't have any of those here." That's where it began—the gauntlet I would run to find my way as a "skier."

My first ski vacation with David was to Taos, N.M. As we walked through the parking lot, I looked for ominous bumper stickers. Luckily, I found none. Unfortunately, above the ticket counter was a full-sized billboard that read "DON'T PANIC!" When I looked up at the mountain, I understood why they didn't leave that message to just bumper stickers. I surreptitiously panicked.

Our second ski trip was to Alta/Snowbird in Utah, where I instituted a practice I would employ for years to come, taking off my skis and walking down the mountain. I have walked down trails at Jay Peak (Vt.), Stowe Mountain Resort (Vt.), Lake Louise (Alberta, Canada), Steamboat (Colo.), Jackson Hole (Wyo.), Grand Targhee (Wyo.), and Telluride (Colo.), to name a few.

I've had oxygen administered at the delightful Swiss restaurant, Alpino Vino (12,000 feet above sea level) in Telluride and then skied my way down. I've panicked on gondolas and cried on chairlifts. I've sat down on steeps and stripped down, completely soaked in the pools of sweat I generated in freezing temperatures as I fought my way down the mountain. I kept coming back for more because I find reservoirs of courage and pockets of joy that have changed me over time. Every minute I ski is a minute I spend on the edge of my comfort zone, pushing and pushing. I don't just ski to become a better skier; I ski to stay outside of my box.

Most recently, after over 10 years of skiing and becoming a solid intermediate skier, I found myself skiing in the Swiss Alps.

"You've got to see this!" I exclaimed, waving trail maps and information pamphlets in the air.

"What?" David asked, not looking up from unpacking his suitcase.

"There is a rotating tram that takes you to the top of the mountain at 10,000 feet where there is a cliff walk, a glacier cave, and a chocolate shop. I'm doing it all! *We're* doing it all. Amazing. And there is sledding! I'm *definitely* sledding."

"I can't believe you're saying this. You don't even sled in Vermont. And a glacier cave? Who are you?" he asked, turning around from the closet where he was hanging shirts.

"Well, it's the new me. You're just not used to me yet. We're doing it all, so get ready," I said sarcastically.

"Oh, I'm ready," he said with a smirk suggesting he'd been born ready, versus me, who had been getting ready for 46 years.

"God! Feel these skis! I can hardly lift them!" I exclaimed, trying to carry my equipment out of the rental shop. I had never rented skis before and felt uneasy trusting someone else's ability to accurately assess my skill level and successfully match it with proper ski equipment.

On the first run, my edges were catching the snow. My mind raced through negative thoughts. "I never should have left my skis at home. That was a huge mistake."

I looked at David and said, "I've ruined this entire week. Why would I rent skis? What was I thinking?!" Tears welled in my eyes.

"It's only your first run," he said. "Give yourself a little time to find your groove. And look, you're crying! That means it's going to be a great day!"

I laughed, knowing he was right. My trajectory was predictable—tears were usually followed by overcoming the fear that caused them and finding my real joy. I charged down what was left of the beginner trail, motivated to jumpstart my progress. Fear, tears, joy, repeat. My week depended on it.

The second run was no better. "Maybe I need some more speed," I said.

"That's the spirit!" David exclaimed, clapping his mittens together. I decided we needed a more intermediate trail.

As I made my way down, I ran through my checkpoints: "Knee bend. Exhale. Grow taller, inhale, pole, and turn. Exhale. Knee bend, inhale, grow …" and then suddenly, my left ski edge caught too early, sending my leg around too fast while my right ski edge dug in and stayed put. Both skis were now moving in opposite directions, and my legs were going with them as I fell forward down the hill. Just before I made contact with the snow, I felt a "pop." My left knee had been pushed too far and couldn't withstand the pressure.

I skidded face-first down the hill until I finally spun around and stopped. I looked up and saw David skiing down toward me, holding one of my poles.

Before we could assess the damage, ski patrol arrived. "Can you ski down?" he asked. I looked at the hill, assessed the pain, and shook my head.

"I will call patrol for a sled, yes?"

By sled, they mean a snowmobile, right? I thought. We waited and waited until ski patrol arrived, not on a snowmobile, but with a toboggan.

"Wait. What?!" I exclaimed. "OK, but I can sit on it like I'm sledding, right?" The patroller introduced himself as "Patrick." He spoke very little English and went right into action, strapping my knee into an air cast and helping me slide on. My head was at the end where the handles extended from the sled. I did the math. I was going down head-first. He put the blankets on top of me, zipped an orange bag around my body, and cinched the straps tight like a straitjacket.

I was starting to panic. Once done, Patrick let me free one hand for "brushing snow off my face" as we traveled downhill. While comforting to have one limb free, the thought of drowning under snow in my face was not.

"Patrick! Patrick!" I yelled. Through my goggles, I saw only blue sky and heard him speaking German to someone on his radio. I needed to know I could take a break to breathe if necessary.

"Patrick! If I yell, will you …" More German. He wasn't listening to me.

I have to get out of here. I'm freaking out! I'm going to die before we even get down. I know it! My thoughts raced, and I continued to yell for him. "Patrick!"

"Patrick, just go and don't stop," David interrupted me, shaking his head and waving his hand toward the bottom of the mountain. "Really. Go, go!" he insisted, waving both hands now.

Patrick skied down the hill holding the sled behind him, and my chest continued to tighten. I was in a full panic attack now and could barely inhale. The only thing I could see was a plane painting a fresh white line on the bright blue sky above me. *Is this worse than flying?* I thought. *It might be worse than flying.*

Then I closed my eyes. I had to find that place deep inside that I had cultivated for years now. It was time.

"Deep breath in and a long breath out." I heard my yoga instructor's voice. Then I raised my free hand to calmly wipe the snow that had pummeled my face.

"Deep breath in. Where are we? Why are we rolling to the left? How much further can it be? Long breath out."

I had no choice but to give up all control to Patrick and completely trust an absolute stranger in my time of need. There was no more fighting that which was saving me.

When we finally stopped, I felt a deep calm wash over me. I felt the sun on my face and had no desire to have him loosen the straps. I could have laid there all day.

"OK?" Patrick asked.

"Yes. I'm OK," I responded with a smile, realizing I was more than OK.

The rest of the day was filled with doctors diagnosing my torn MCL and thoughts of what the rest of my week would look like. I named my brace Yoda because I knew this experience had something to teach me. I found new ways to move around. I tried to stay positive by repeating Deepak Chopra's mantra that only misery comes from trying to change what is, but it grew more difficult to manage my mental state over the next few days because I wanted so much more. I could have used this as the perfect excuse to just shop, spa, and drink champagne all day, but I actually wanted some adventure.

By day three of the brace, I stayed in bed as David left for a full day of backcountry skiing. The pain and swelling were increasing daily, and moving around was exhausting, both mentally and physically. But I decided to shower for the first time since our arrival, determined to get out of that room and find some adventure.

As I combed my hair, I saw a person in the mirror staring back at me I didn't quite recognize. I suddenly remembered being back in that hotel room in Utah with Greg so many years before. I remembered him walking out the door and the paralysis I felt in staying. My inability to escape those four walls because of the overwhelming fear of failure and judgment, whether it was because I couldn't ski or breathe.

I didn't recognize that woman anymore. I had come so far in the choices I'd made, from small steps to large leaps—all the way to Switzerland to see just how far out of that box I had come. Here I was now, no more walls blocking the sun from shining on me, illuminating who I had become on the other side.

I was physically unable to move faster than an ambitious sloth. I was nauseous from either the trauma or the strange food or both. But I was leaving my hotel room all alone for an unknown adventure that awaited me on the outside of those walls. I had only a map, a lift pass, and a credit card, and I did as much as I possibly could.

I soared to the mountain peaks, explored the glacier cave, and wrote on sun-drenched decks watching gondolas pass by. I sipped cappuccinos and felt the sun on my face at an outdoor café. I ate heavenly goat cheese at 8,000 feet above sea level and chatted with children from Glasgow, whose only concerns were Coca-Cola and bubble gum.

These may not sound like adventures to you, and I would agree. They are not. The adventure was leaving the box in the first place and allowing the Universe to unfold around me.

Driving

For my 40th birthday, I asked to go to Las Vegas and drive exotic cars. I took the training class, strapped on my helmet, and drove a Porsche 911 Turbo S, a Ferrari 458 Italia, and an Audi R8. I loved every minute of it. Five years later, David and I signed up for a weekend driving event in Mont Tremblant, Quebec, where we could drive our own car on a racetrack.

As a beginner, I was assigned to group D, which required having a driving instructor ride with me as I ran my laps. My instructor was in group A. He was an expert.

"I read that the fastest way to learn is to ride shotgun in a car with a group A driver," David said over dinner the night before we started.

"I will never do that. That's just insane. I realize doing this in the first place is outside my box, but at least I'm driving, and it's with other novices on the track. What you're suggesting means I have zero control over the car, and I'm on the track with others driving a million miles an hour. There is no way in hell I would ever do that. Nope."

The more I said no, the more I heard *"well, maybe"* in the back of my mind. I smirked to myself, thinking, *Here we go again.* The next morning, we arrived at the track to find we didn't have enough gas to get through the day. David looked at the schedule. His group was driving second and mine was third, so he had time to rush out to find a nearby gas station.

"Wait! Gimme the helmet before you leave. I need to wear it around the parking lot to get comfortable," I said.

The event rules mandated that all drivers wear full-face helmets. It was so claustrophobic that I was truly panicked about wearing it. It had kept me up at night and almost caused me to cancel the entire trip. As he drove off, I took a deep breath, closed my eyes, and squeezed my head into what felt like a birth canal. I paced around for a bit, trying to breathe, reminding myself I could take it off at any time. Eventually, I found my instructor and introduced myself. While he had never seen anyone just walking around the parking lot in a helmet before, he got it once I explained my circumstances.

"Group A is going out first this morning. Do you want to come? My passenger's seat is empty, and it would be a good introduction to the track for you."

I looked at his car. It was a real race car. The inside was stripped, and the seats had full harnesses. I was incredibly intimidated.

Shit! I thought. *Here it is—where the rubber hits the road, literally.* I pulled off the helmet to give my brain space to think.

"Umm. My husband just drove off with my long sleeve shirt," I said—another event rule. *Genius!* I thought as I shrugged. Perfect excuse and not my fault.

"My girlfriend brought an extra. She'd be fine with you borrowing it."

Shit, shit, SHIT! I thought. Then I said, "Ya. Sure. I'll go." *Pause.* "How many times have you driven this track again?"

"Tons," he laughed, sensing my hesitation as he helped strap me into my harness. There was no going back now. I focused on my breath while he talked me through every gear shift, every turn, and every lane change. I took it all in, watching the cars pass and memorizing the course.

When it was over, we motored slowly back to his parking spot, and I saw David standing at our car, smiling. I feverishly unbuckled, swung the car door open, and ran toward him, yelling, "That was amazing!" As I hugged him, I realized I was still wearing the helmet. I had completely forgotten about it. "I can't believe I did that," I said, panting.

"Never, huh? Didn't take you long this time," he smirked.

I smiled wide and buzzed with endorphins. I felt invigorated and empowered. That ride changed everything for me. I experienced the entire weekend from a place of excitement—wanting and doing more, rather than watching from behind a barrier and staying inside my comfort zone. I leaned in and made it my own. I used my fear as fuel and rode the wave of adrenaline. I lived it rather than watched it.

The Diagnosis

When a diagnosis determines your fate,
without any debate.
Without asking permission,
without hope of remission.
Only faith keeps your head above water.
Only the love of your son and your daughters.
Only the strength of a husband and sister.
Only expressing how much we will miss her.
Only prayers that the suffering will cease.
Only then a sacred passing in peace.

Chapter 38

The Lifeline Lost

"Yes, Mother. I can see you are flawed. You have not hidden it.
That is your greatest gift to me."
—Alice Walker

A CONSTANT STREAM of Christmas packages had started arriving at the house. As soon as Thanksgiving dinner was digested, the online ordering began. FedEx, UPS, and the U.S. Postal Service became daily visitors in December. Each package held a gift for someone I loved.

Meanwhile, Christmas cards poured in from family and friends, along with small gifts left in the mailbox by neighbors. While stressful, Christmas is still a magical time, a sacred time when I feel safe and loved.

The Monday before Christmas, I received four Christmas cards, three UPS packages, two FedEx boxes, and one phone call. It was 5:10 p.m. I walked into David's office, looked into his eyes, and said, "My mother has cancer." And then I cried. It felt natural, like what I should be doing in that moment, but I was completely numb. I had just enough time to wipe the tears and blow my nose for my stepdaughter's holiday choral concert.

David and I sat in a dark auditorium watching grade school children sing holiday carols with angelic voices and awkward hand gestures. Music triggers such strong memories that I was transported to the couch I grew up with, sitting with my mother enjoying the sight of our decorated tree, listening to holiday music, and talking for hours. The tears were too fresh to hold back during the final medley of Christmas classics, and my one tissue was grossly inadequate. The minute I gave up the battle and thought, "At least the lights are off," the overhead lights came on, and the choral director invited the audience to sing along by yelling, "Everyone!"

Grief doesn't take a holiday.

At first, I felt all the things that are disclosed as potential side effects on common prescription drugs: nausea, dizziness, swelling of the throat, headache, diarrhea, difficulty concentrating, and a sense that operating heavy machinery was not a good idea. Then I went into battle mode when we were given the final diagnosis of metastatic stage IV pancreatic cancer, along with two printouts of possible clinical trials, and sent on our way.

The next two weeks were hell. The cancer community in the United States has extreme deficiencies in serving its patients. Even patients who are highly educated and tenacious struggle to navigate the system. What does that mean for the patients with language barriers or patients without the tools or time to search complex websites written in medical jargon? You die of cancer while waiting on hold to talk to someone who will eventually confirm they know nothing about the clinical trial you are calling about even though their phone number is listed on the government website. You die of cancer while researching clinical trials on your own because of inadequate staffing at oncologist offices and cancer centers and running into dead end after dead end while you delay chemotherapy because the trials require that you come in without any prior treatment. This pressure to find all of your viable options, collect all relevant information, and make a well-informed decision on care and therapy while the clock is ticking and the cancer is spreading is unbearable.

Moving through this process, I felt numb. I was in a dark tunnel where my normal world was muted in both sight and sound. My senses were insulated by the gravity of the diagnosis, impenetrable by normal joys like fresh flowers or a night out. I sat staring off into nowhere with no feelings or thoughts. It was the space between no cancer diagnosis and rejecting a death sentence.

Whenever I was met with the reality of the situation for only a moment, the tears would flow. It was not the crying I felt on that first day I heard the news. That was conscious. I acknowledged the tears, gave them permission, and felt them wash down my face. Now I had no control. If I gave in to a moment of making eye contact with the diagnosis, the pain, the inevitability, my chest tightened, my stomach dropped, and then I realized tears were running down my face only after the spigot was completely open. Involuntary weeping. I couldn't find a conscious shelf for death to sit on. I could only feel it lingering in my body, looking for a home.

I've always said that I would not be able to handle the death of my parents. While Jack Kornfield, the meditation guru, says, "Acknowledge the tears you carry," my first reaction was to ignore, deny, and keep moving. Do I hold it together for those around me, or do I fall apart the way any child in my position would? Do I fall apart now before she dies to get it over with, or wait and see if I ever need to go there?

I think that every person interprets the concept of closure differently based on their personal experiences and relationships. I had tried to achieve the closure I was looking for two years prior at a dinner with my parents and sister. It was two days before Christmas, and I wanted all of us to acknowledge some things I believed happened in the past. Events that caused me pain and were the source of much of my anxiety. I thought these events created a common history among us all that we could share and move past. I was looking for connection but was met with opposition on so many levels. No one at that table wanted to revisit the memories I had or acknowledged their validity. Regardless of the bad timing, I realized my past and my truth were not theirs.

What did closure mean two months before my mother's death? I used to believe that childhood wounds that are never properly tended to create scars that last a lifetime. But do we need to cut those scars back open and watch them bleed to have them heal? Will that provide closure, or is it merely an assignment of blame, a demand for acknowledgment, or an apology? Is that really what I needed?

Alice says in Wonderland, "It's no use going back to yesterday because I was a different person then." I took that to heart. Not just that I was a different person then, but so was my mother.

In my search for closure before she died, rather than stir up old memories and cut open old wounds, I chose to forgive the version of my mother that no longer existed and acknowledge that the old version was doing the best she could at the time. I knew she was sorry now without having to replay the tapes and relive the pain.

What I felt in my heart I gave as a gift to the 6-year-old version of myself who was still holding onto those memories in order to heal her wounds. My mother is no longer that person any more than I am that little girl. So rather than have a painful conversation about the baggage I still carried, I chose to drop the bags and free up my arms to embrace the woman in front of me and love her with action and intention. I spent my time with her making sure that everything I did and said expressed how much I loved her.

Four months after the first phone call, another call came. It was my sister calling from a hospital room in Florida. What had been a routine visit to make sure my mother wasn't having another allergic reaction to the chemotherapy turned into an end that came too soon. I packed my bags and boarded a plane with a one-way ticket, not knowing when I would return home.

"You came," she said, holding out her shaking hand.

"Of course I came," I replied, tears streaming down my face.

"Don't cry. Why … are you … crying?" Her speech was slow and slurred.

"Because I'm happy to see you." I sat down in the chair next to her bed and took her hand in mine. She was wearing a knit hat that would fall lower and lower on her head as the life drained from her body over the next three days.

Her eyes closed slowly for a moment, and when she opened them again, they lit up as if she was seeing me for the first time.

"I've been in here for over two days now. I have to get out. Please get me out. I have to go home." She looked pained as she pulled at the bed linens.

"We are talking to the doctors and will get you home as soon as we can. I promise. I know it's uncomfortable. Are you in pain?" I asked.

She nodded slowly as her eyes closed again. Without letting go of her hand, I asked my sister to find the nurse.

"I'm so glad you came," she said, her eyes open again. I knew that she thought I would be able to get her out of that hospital and back home. To this day, I can't shake the pain I felt not having been able to do that—to save her. The pain I felt knowing that I had flown halfway across the country to help convince my father that it was time to move her into the hospice facility.

"Of course, I came. I love you. Jim is on his way, too. So, everyone will be here together this afternoon." My brother was on a plane and wouldn't arrive in time to have one last conversation with her like this. Mine would be her last.

I assured her over and over again that we would be taking her home as soon as possible. I knew it was a lie but hoped that when we moved her to the hospice facility, the morphine and anti-anxiety medications would create enough of a fog that she might actually think she was home.

The last time she closed her eyes, it lasted longer than just a moment, so I closed mine, too. I felt her fragile hand in mine. I knew this body was not all that was left of my mother. I imagined her soul, her spirit, her essence separating from her physical body and trying to meet her there somewhere above that bed and beyond the physical. I silently talked to her, spirit to spirit, soul to soul. I believed she could hear and feel me. When I opened my eyes, she looked peacefully asleep. This became my only way to communicate with her over the next three days.

That afternoon, we signed papers agreeing to stop administering her food. In all of the discussions around end-of-life care, this had never been discussed, and it didn't feel right to take away her strength to fight a little longer. But the hospice nurses explained the protocol and assured us it was for the best. Regardless, it still felt like signing a death warrant.

All that was left to do was wait for someone in the hospice facility to die so a room would become available. The next morning, we got the news and moved her from the hospital to a hospice room across town. It was all becoming too real, too final, too fast. We all sat vigil at her bedside, watching and waiting for signs of life or lucidity, signs of pain or anxiety. We played her favorite TV shows and music in the background. We talked about favorite memories and Christmases, and we watched each other's hearts breaking around us.

We all gathered for dinner each night to find strength again to go back into that room for another day. After three days passed, at the advice of the nurses, my sister and I told my father it was important for him to spend time alone with her. He needed to let her know it was OK for her to pass and that he would be fine. When he walked out of the room crying, I knew he needed a break. I gathered my things and took him and my brother to get some lunch. My sister stayed behind, turned on my mother's favorite TV show, and sat by her bedside.

Just minutes down the road, my cellphone rang.

"You need to come back."

"What?" I couldn't understand her through the crying.

"She's gone! You need to come back now," she shouted through the sniffling.

I don't let myself walk back into those rooms very often. They both hold memories that still shatter my core. My lifeline, my mother, slipped beneath the surface as I stood there, powerless, only able to watch.

You think death is an unfortunate reality affecting others until it comes knocking on your door and says, "It's time." Death is inevitable for every living thing. Death can come suddenly or slowly over time. Many of our common fears originate from our overwhelming fear of death because we know how closely it waits in the wings.

Watching the life drain from my mother those last three days was my worst nightmare come true. There was nowhere to run from it and no waking up from it. It's a clear memory etched onto my heart and a part of me forever. And it's a shared memory that my father, sister, and brother will all carry. Like the cancer diagnosis, I haven't found a place to put that loss yet. Unlike fitting a body into a casket, my heart wasn't big enough to absorb that much pain, and it overflowed through the tears I continue to shed.

The grieving process is complicated. When I was young and watched my parents fight, I viewed my mother's rage, tears, and accusations as the source of the problem. I blamed her for the pain I saw my father go through. I wanted to save him from her, but I didn't know how. I did everything I could to not make it worse. I tried to be perfect.

Watching my father hold her hand and whisper under his breath through the tears triggered those memories again. I saw the pain she was causing him, and I couldn't do anything about it. The clinical trial research, the ceaseless communications with doctors, nothing I did would be enough to buy time. The wigs and new wardrobe we bought when she was wasting away from chemo-induced anorexia was a mere distraction, a cosmetic alteration that lifted her spirit while her cancer remained unphased. But I didn't blame her this time. It was just death, and it was tragic.

But as I sat there looking at her in that bed, something washed away the stains of the past, and I saw only a soul in a shell. No baggage. It was as if the weight she had shed from the chemo was the pain from a life lived in anguish and chaos at times. The weight of regret and loss. It was all suddenly gone, and all I saw was the raw material and pure love. In those moments, closure was no longer something I sought but something sacred I felt in my heart as the scars of old wounds disappeared. I felt only the purest love I had ever experienced.

Watching your lifeline die unsettles the soul. It moved me to stand a little straighter, breathe a little deeper, and recognize the strength I had been harboring for years. I was on my own now, but the reality was, I had always been alone. I could now see the irony that she was both the cause of the pain and my savior from it. In forgiving her, I found my own heart's path to healing, wholeness, and love.

Chapter 39

The Breadcrumbs

"My barn having burned down,
I can now see the moon."
—Mizuta Masahide
(17th c. Japanese poet and samurai)

JUST AS MEDITATION and yoga are practices, so is staying outside my box. Because even though I found my way out, there is always a trail of breadcrumbs leading me back in. The more I practice, the less power those breadcrumbs have over me.

While on this journey to make sense of those stars—those pieces of me—scattered across the night sky, I was faced with anxiety in ways I never thought I'd have to confront again. The pull of the box became stronger than ever. As I entered those caves I feared the most and revisited certain struggles, it was as if I was transported back in time to either experience the anxiety so intensely again so I could share it on these pages or heal a wound that was still open.

While facing my first bout with depression and dissociative disorder in the fifth grade and my suicidal episode in college, I noticed that I was looking at it all from a very safe distance—from the outside looking in. I was terrified of going back into that fog for fear that I may not find my way back out.

I was writing about it and thinking about it on the surface, and I knew it. The work required that I do more, that I enter that cave now years later and face that dragon again, but I couldn't find the entrance.

That night I went to a candlelight yoga class. I picked a spot in the front row corner with just two large pillar candles in front of me and a painted wall. As the class progressed, I found myself feeling dizzy. At first, I attributed it to doing balance poses and twists in such dim light. But as it continued, a twinge of anxiety came over me. It brought me back to walking around my apartment in Connecticut with vertigo that would last for weeks and the added layer of fog it created. I pushed the thoughts away as quickly as they had rushed in, feeling twinges of panic stir in my belly.

I left class still dizzy and getting progressively more uneasy about it. What was happening to me? Was it more than a dimly lit room? I didn't tell anyone as I progressed through my evening, convincing myself it would be gone in the morning. When I woke, I had that familiar few minutes upon rising when I forgot anything could be wrong, but when I looked in the bathroom mirror, it all came rushing back, just like my past fogs decades ago. I struggled to get through my morning routine, forgetting what task came next. I couldn't recall what my plan for the day was or what I was working on.

I decided to run some errands in hopes that doing something I had done every day for years would help me get my bearings. On my ride home, I thought, *OK, this still hasn't passed. I am slipping deeper into this fog, and I'm not sure I'm equipped to deal with it. David has never even seen me like this in the 10 years we've been together. The only positive that can come of it is to go home and write. Write it all down.*

And that's exactly what I did. I sat deep in the fog, and I wrote and wrote. I wrote about every feeling and fear that was pulsing through my veins. They weren't the same fears from years past, but the fog was just thick enough to suck me right back in. I was in the cave, and with no weapons or armor except a pen and paper, I explored all of its dark corners and sharp edges. When I emerged, I shared what I wrote with David.

"Wow. I've never seen you in this condition or heard anything like that before," he said.

"I know. I haven't been there in over 15 years, and then last night it returned and led me back to that place inexplicably," I responded.

And with that, it was gone.

Another episode was in Vermont when I awoke to plenty of snow and extremely cold temperatures hovering just below 0° Fahrenheit. David suggested taking advantage of the cross-country skiing in our yard with the house close by to keep us warm if needed. I agreed wholeheartedly and bundled up to break some trails once the needle rose above zero.

It was as if someone sprinkled glitter over the entire yard as the sunlight illuminated the snow crystals. The clouds were perfect orbs of cotton flirting with the tips of the mountains as they floated through the bright blue sky.

Once I started skiing, my body felt warm but tight, and I could feel my brows clenching together. Under all of my gear, I wore a scowl on my face. I thought I could shake it by stopping to take a photo and appreciate the majesty of the day, filling my heart with gratitude, but the negativity welled up deep inside me and seeped out of my pores. I felt completely separate from where I was.

Why? I thought. *What is going on? I want to absorb every bit of this glorious time communing with nature and being with David, yet I can't feel any of it.* Something was gnawing away at me from the inside out.

The snow was so deep that my skis were sinking in about a foot below the surface as I cut new tracks. My first pass around the house was not easy, so I decided not to venture off that track once made. I saw David in the distance cutting other tracks through a sparsely wooded area, then out onto the open field and down to the bottom of a hill and through a row of tight trees that led into an even more densely wooded area on the edge of our property.

I typically ski through those woods when there is much less snow to fight, and I enter from the open, flat field at the bottom of the hill. I don't ever enter through a line of trees while skiing down a hill, gaining speed. My first thought was, "I know he's going to want me to do that." My *second* thought was, "Never."

I was imagining myself at the bottom of the hill in the woods in two feet of snow—it would be nearly impossible to herringbone my skis in such deep snow to dig my way out. My resistance was mounting at the thought of it.

"Babe, you should come try this. It's really amazing," he called as I completed my third loop around the house on high ground.

I told him I had no interest and gave him a thousand reasons why it made no sense to me.

"I'm just uncomfortable."

"I think you'll be surprised at how slow and manageable it is given how much snow there is," he replied.

"I have no interest in aiming my skies downhill at a row of trees," I said emphatically. "Not to mention all the extra snow in the woods. I'd suffocate!"

"There isn't more snow in the woods, and I've already carved the trail."

I just stared back at him, thinking, *He just doesn't get it.*

He looked down and shook his head with disappointment. He could feel my resistance and was confused by my response, given all the work he had watched me do growing outside my box. He knew there was something else going on.

I skied past him and continued my loops, two of which I spent thinking, *Nothing is ever enough for him. It's not enough that I'm out here, and it's only five degrees. He always has to push me to do more or try something new, and I just can't. I want to do what I know and what is safe. That's how I enjoy things. No stress, no surprises, no risk.* My eyes were burning as I buried the tears.

Enough about him. Let's think about something else, so that doesn't ruin my time out here, I thought. I started thinking about the book and found myself wondering why I was writing it if I was still stuck like this. I wasn't even enjoying my conservative, safe loop around the house, never mind playing outside my comfort zone.

The defeatist voice grew louder and louder, and in my mind's eye, I could see an angry face growing more and more enraged like the face of the Wizard. I remember thinking about how my mother's face got distorted when she was enraged, and in this moment, the face reminded me of her. It was as if the more I questioned, the angrier she became. And then the little girl appeared and claimed the voice as her own. She wasn't happy that I'd done so much work and had taken back so much control. It was as if my own resistance had re-awakened her, giving her a spark of hope or a tiny crack to seep back in.

I felt overwhelmed and wanted to turn away, but this little girl was a part of me. How could I be so afraid of myself? There was no place to run. I felt unsettled deep in my core, as if she was trying to take back control again. Despite the sun shining all around me, I was suddenly in a very dark place.

"Who do you think you are? Why are you trying to quiet me? Why are you telling other people about me? Why do you think anyone will care?" I felt the power shifting back and forth. It was like a full Star Wars, light versus dark, good versus evil moment, except she wasn't evil—she was still scared. Deep in my heart, I knew. I had to see her in a different light, yet the image haunted me as I continued my loop. I couldn't break free from it.

I skied until I saw David clipping out of his skis in the garage. It had been close to two hours, and we were both ready for lunch. While resting on the couch, he said, "I didn't think you'd stay out that long."

"My only goal was to stay out as long as you. If you could stand the cold, then I could, too."

"That was my goal! Once I saw you get in your groove, I figured I'd stay out as long as you were finding your joy. But I had to use the bathroom, so I went in and was ready to go back out if you were still at it," he replied.

We broke into laughter. "We could have been out there for days if neither of us stopped!" I said. Little did he know I had not found my joy and was still feeling uneasy with that image lingering in my mind.

"I'll go back out again tonight before sunset if we have time," I said. He agreed.

As we moved through the rest of our day, I felt a pull to get back on my skis. Something was calling me back out there; something was unfinished. The first two hours were so uncomfortable that I didn't really want to, but I had to.

When we arrived back home, I quickly unpacked groceries from the car and changed my clothes.

"You're going back out?" David asked.

"Of course. Less than 90 minutes till sunset," I replied, pulling my thickest socks up to my knees. The temperature was dropping again, so I didn't know how long I would last. But I knew I needed to get back out there.

I booted up and kissed him on the cheek, "I'll see ya when I see ya." When we started at different times, you could ski for hours without seeing the other person.

My first loop on the high ground was fine, but I could feel myself longing for more. On my next lap, I headed into the sparsely wooded area that had a slight downhill slope. I was able to control my speed by pushing one ski out of the track and into the heavier snow. I took a sharp left turn at the end to exit back onto the open field where the slope steepened. I could head across the hill back to my loop or toward the line of trees that marked the opening to the woods at the edge of our property. I looked down the hill and considered a more gentle approach. I turned my skis down the hill and zig-zagged back and forth across it to slow my speed. At the very end, I turned onto the trail through a space just wide enough for my body to fit through the trees.

Having no idea what I would find in there, my heart raced. To my pleasant surprise, rather than finding more snow beneath my feet and hanging in the trees around me, I found a well-broken trail and a canopy of trees covered in white crystals that glistened like Christmas ornaments in the sunbeams that filtered through the branches. I skied through to the open field on the other side and paused at the very bottom of the hill. I didn't feel like I was drowning or helpless. I found the track David had broken and skied straight up it with no backsliding.

I did that loop over and over and over again. All the while, the hills were getting faster as the snow compacted under my skis. My zig zag became an s-curve that became a straight line down the hill through the trees and into the glorious woods. My traverse up the hill became a satisfying burn in my thighs that empowered my spirit, as if I was making up for every time I cried to be carried at the end of a sled run.

I passed David several times as he cut back branches in different sections of the woods to break new trails. As the sun set, I watched the sky turn apricot over the mountains and the bright blue of day turn to a light gray that whispered to me, "Good work today."

I'd found my way back from the crippling fear and limitations of the morning to the open mind and heart of the evening. I moved away from my resistance and leaned into the need to test my boundaries and find what lay beyond the edge of the woods. I stared down that part of me that pulled me back to the box and reached out my hand to invite her along for the ride, taking care of her along the way.

I couldn't force it in the morning just because David asked me to. I had to find my own path there.

I had been skiing for two hours, and it was well past sunset. The darkness was closing in around me, but I fearlessly skied past the house for one more cycle.

"Try my new trail in there," he yelled from the garage, taking off his skis. I had seen him clipping branches next to the first downhill trail in the woods.

"Maybe," I replied with a Cheshire grin. I entered the woods and came to the fork where I could choose the path to the left that I had taken 15 times before, or the path to the right that he had just cut. I could see clearly where my path exited onto the open field while the end of his path was out of sight. I turned my skis to the right and pushed off with my poles as hard as I could. The path twisted and turned until I reached a spot so tight that my body barely fit through the trees, and I needed to step over barbed wire lying in the snow from an old property line fence. It finally dumped me into the lower woods, so the trails were now all connected.

I felt exhilarated and even more alive as I headed into the densest part of the woods with barely any light. I felt safe and calm—in complete harmony with nature—as if I could lay down and sleep there for the night.

As I emerged back onto the open field at the bottom of the hill, I skied in the line of a perfect moonbeam shining off the snow. I tilted my head up to feel its glow engulf me. I felt a pure wholeness, at one with myself and the world around me. I found my joy and peace.

About a month later, I was contemplating how my journey would end. Would there be something significant to mark the occasion or just more opening over time? I meditated and was immediately brought back to where it all began. I was standing in front of a quiet Wizard and saw the little girl standing behind the half-pulled curtain.

I reached out my hand, and she stepped toward me and let me embrace her. I closed my eyes and felt the energy build between us. I felt no tension or conflict, only love and a deep sense of wholeness.

When I opened my eyes, she was gone. I felt the air grow damp and saw green leaves and vines draped around me. Then I heard it. The waterfall rushing in the distance. I was going back to see the women.

When I arrived, they guided me into the water. I stepped in alone and faced the circle. This pool of collected tears was now where I stood in my peace. I closed my eyes and leaned my head back under the rushing water. All of the pain in those tears that washed over me now felt like power. In that moment, I owned my hard-fought freedom and stood in my truth.

When I opened my eyes, it was so bright I could hardly make out the women. Then as quickly as my eyes adjusted, they each disappeared in a brilliant burst until there was *nothing left but light*.

"She remembered who she was, and the game changed."
—*Lalah Delia*

Endnotes

[1]Anxiety and Depression Association of America (ADAA); https://adaa.org/understanding-anxiety/facts-statistics#:~:text=Anxiety%20disorders%20affect%20 25.1%25%20of,and%20engage%20in%20substance%20abuse; December 12, 2019

[2]ibid

[3]https://www.verywellmind.com/what-is-the-fight-or-flight-response-2795194; December 12, 2019

[4]https://adaa.org/understanding-anxiety/generalized-anxiety-disorder-gad - March 14, 2021

[5]https://adaa.org/understanding-anxiety/panic-disorder - March 14, 2021

[6]https://adaa.org/understanding-anxiety/facts-statistics#:~:text=affected%20 as%20men.-,Social%20Anxiety%20Disorder,more%20years%20before%20seek ing%20help - March 14, 2021

[7]https://adaa.org/understanding-anxiety/facts-statistics#:~:text=Crisis%20 (Oct%202020)-,Obsessive%2DCompulsive%20Disorder%20(OCD),first%20 experienced%20symptoms%20in%20childhood - March 14, 2021

[8]https://www.nimh.nih.gov/health/statistics/suicide.shtml - March 14, 2021

[9]https://www.ncbi.nlm.nih.gov/pubmed/11728849. - December 12, 2019

[10]https://namica.org/illnesses/dissociative-disorders/ - March 14, 2021

[11]https://www.betterhelp.com/advice/personality-disorders/depersonalization -derealization-disorder-what-to-expect-symptoms-and-treatment/ - March 14, 2021

[12]https://www.healthline.com/health/depersonalization-disorder - December 12, 2019

[13]https://www.mayoclinic.org/diseases-conditions/depersonalization-derealization-disorder/symptoms-causes/syc-20352911 - December 12, 2019

[14]ibid

[15]https://www.nami.org/About-Mental-Illness/Mental-Health-Conditions/Dissociative-Disorders - December 12, 2019

[16]https://www.medicalnewstoday.com/articles/316427#insulin-glucagon-and-blood-sugar - December 12, 2019

[17]https://ibpf.org/are-you-a-perfectionist-bipolar-and-perfectionism-may-go-hand-in-hand/#:~:text=%E2%80%9CPerfectionistic%20people%20typically%20believe%20that,Greenspon. - March 30, 2020

[18]https://theanthrotorian.com/art/2012/10/16/michelangelos-slaves - June 12, 2019

[19]ibid

[20]The 5-4-3-2-1 technique involves finding 5 things to stimulate one sense (e.g., Look at 5 things), then find 4 things to stimulate a different sense (e.g., smell 4 things), then find 3 things to stimulate another sense (e.g., touch 3 things), then 2 (e.g., listen to 2 things) and finally 1 (taste 1 thing).

[21]Mark Nepo, Super Soul Conversations, OWN, "We either willfully shed or break open." TV Show.

[22]https://www.merriam-webster.com/dictionary/crucible - March 30, 2020.

[23]Sting, Nothing Like the Sun released on 13 October 1987 on A&M Records.

About the author

Wendy Tamis Robbins is an attorney, author, speaker, anxiety coach, and self-proclaimed professional "panic-attacker." After living with various anxiety and panic disorders for almost 40 years, she is now anxiety-free. Not because she is entirely free of anxiety, but because it no longer controls her. She has traded living in resistance for building resilience. Her fears now fuel a life not only beyond her diagnosis but beyond her dreams.

On her path to recovery, she discovered a restorative, inner peace and reclaimed her authentic power. She is passionate about helping others who are hiding their fears behind destructive perfectionism and accommodating their anxiety to find the same freedom.

When Wendy hit rock bottom, it was hearing other people's stories that saved her life. Now she shares her own to be an example of what's possible.

Her unique coaching draws from her personal experience while finding common and relatable ground. Her balanced approach utilizes practical thought and holistic body/mind work while keeping a sharp focus on the goal. By allowing you to imagine your most beautiful life beyond anxiety, Wendy shows you how to believe it can be true, decide you are worthy of it, and ultimately manifest it.

Despite her anxiety, Wendy earned a scholarship and worked her way through Dartmouth College, where she competed on the varsity track and field team. After graduating from law school, she began her career as a corporate tax and finance attorney, working to create and preserve affordable housing and provide social impact financing and public welfare investments to underserved communities. She and her husband, David, live on the Massachusetts North Shore with his two teenage children. Wendy enjoys tennis, skiing, yoga, cycling, traveling, and race car driving.

CPSIA information can be obtained
at www.ICGtesting.com
Printed in the USA
JSHW050233260521
15121JS00002B/2

9 781641 466226